BRUCE TRAIL

AN ADVENTURE
ALONG THE NIAGARA
ESCARPMENT

BRUCE TRAIL

AN ADVENTURE ALONG THE NIAGARA ESCARPMENT

by Rich and Sue Freeman

Footprint Press
Fishers, New York, 14453
www.footprintpress.com

Other books available from
Footprint Press include:

Take A Hike! Family Walks in the Rochester (NY) Area

Take Your Bike! Family Rides in the Rochester (NY) Area

Alter - A Simple Path to Emotional Wellness

Manufactured and published in the United States of America
Footprint Press, P.O. Box 645, Fishers NY, USA 14453
(www.footprintpress.com)

Edited by Diane Maggs
Cover by Image and Eye Graphics Services
Photographs and Maps by Rich and Sue Freeman

Cataloging-in-Publication Data

796.5   Freeman, Richard (Richard Earl), 1949, Mar. 13-
FRE   Bruce Trail : An Adventure Along the Niagara Escarpment /
       by Rich & Sue Freeman.-Fishers, N.Y. : Footprint Press, ©1998.

       224 p. : ill., maps ; cm.
       Includes index.

       Summary: Describes a 5-week backpacking journey along
       the Bruce Trail in Ontario, Canada, highlighting the flora and
       fauna of the region and providing survival tips and techniques
       for long-distance backpacking.

       ISBN 0-9656974-3-6
       LCCN: 97-078231

       1. Hiking - Bruce Trail (Ont.) - Guidebooks 2. Trails-
       Ontario - Guidebooks 3. Bruce Trail (Ont.) - Guidebooks
       1. Freeman, Susan (Susan Joy), 1953 Feb. 12-   II.Title

GV199.42   796.5'1'09713_dc21

       Provided in cooperation with Unique Books, Inc.

Dedication

This book is dedicated, with our sincere appreciation, to:

- The volunteers of the Bruce Trail Association whose hard labor and perseverance resulted in the creation and maintenance of this spectacular trail.

- The landowners who let us and all other hikers walk gently across their private lands.

- Sue's parents, Joyce and Harold Connor, who once again formed our home support crew. Without their assistance we wouldn't be free to wander the great trails of the world.

Acknowledgments

Whenever you're on a backpacking trip—without a car in today's society—you're at the mercy of others for assistance. Our heartfelt thanks are extended to the many people who helped us along the way on our Bruce Trail adventure. Many of them are named in this book. They gave us rides, fed us, filled our water bottles, provided shelter, and offered words of encouragement along the way.

Others helped with the production of the book itself and are just as valued. Jaci Winters, Pat Stainton, and Bruce Calvert from the Bruce Trail Association provided information and read our manuscript for accuracy. Our good friend Bob Fordyce read the manuscript to assure us that it was readable. Amy Amish of Image and Eye Graphics Services designed our cover, and Diane Maggs made sure that our grammar was correct.

The Bruce Trail

Contents

Introduction

The Bruce Trail meanders for approximately 465 miles (800 km) following the rocky spine of the Niagara Escarpment. It is the oldest long-distance walking path in Canada, celebrating its thirty-year anniversary in the year of our hike (1997). As we sprint toward a new millennium, over a million people a year now explore the Bruce Trail, the majority for day hikes. A ribbon of urban wilderness, the Bruce Trail begins at Queenston Heights, just north of Niagara Falls, crosses the Welland Canal, skirts Stoney Creek and Hamilton, and bursts upon the hills and fields northwest of Toronto, passing through some of the most populated areas of Ontario Province. It winds its way toward Georgian Bay, which is sometimes called the sixth Great Lake. With views of stark white cliffs, cobblestone beaches, and azure seas, it climbs the Bruce Peninsula then ends as the escarpment dives majestically underwater at Tobermory.

It took us five weeks to walk from end to end, carrying all we needed on our backs. Many people think we're crazy for giving up the status of corporate executive jobs and a comfortable home to wander in the woods and live in a tent. But backpacking has a lure that calls to us louder than the honking horns of a traffic jam on our rush to work. Backpacking gets the blood coursing through our veins as we push to climb hill after hill. The physical exertion rejuvenates our souls. We feel instant gratification as we stand on a ledge and look back over the terrain just covered, seeing where we were just a few hours ago. It's amazing how far we can go, one footstep at a time. Wandering through the woods at a walking pace, we have time to notice the flora and fauna. We can watch spring leaves unfold or fall colors become brighter day by day. We discover new ferns and see sights that most people never see from their air-conditioned cars and fenced in yards. For us, backpacking is the ultimate in freedom and what better place to be free than on the beautiful Bruce Trail along the Niagara Escarpment.

As free as we feel wandering the countryside, we owe a debt of gratitude to the people who form our logistical support team. For this trip we had two sets of assistants. My parents, Joyce and Harold Connor, left their Florida home to live in our house while we were gone. They tended to our animals, maintained our "For Sale" home for browsers, and kept our publishing business alive. My cousins, Cathy and Ray Neal, drove us to the start of the trail, stored our van in their Stoney Creek driveway, and graciously opened their home to us before, for a pit stop during, and at the end of our trek. A loving family allows us to be free in body as well as in spirit.

Rich and I have grown into hiking. We started with neighborhood walks, getting involved at the grass roots level with a local volunteer group to develop a network of hiking trails in our neighborhood. In 1996, we walked away from corporate jobs to spend six months hiking the Appalachian Trail, which runs from Georgia to Maine in the United States. That was Rich's first backpacking trip and a phenomenal accomplishment for both of us. We look back on it now and wonder how we ever made it the whole way. I think it was plain stubbornness. Once we commit to something, we carry it through to the end. It was also a life-changing experience. Neither of us could face returning to the corporate world, and we wanted to find a way to get more people involved in the joy of hiking.

We spent the winter of 1996-1997 researching and writing a book on hiking trails around Rochester, New York. *Take A Hike! Family Walks In The Rochester Area* was well received and a barrel of fun. It inspired us to continue down this path.

In this book, we share our journal so you can experience the Bruce Trail trek along with us. We also share our accumulated knowledge on the art of backpacking. Hopefully, it will inspire you to venture out and experience your own freedom. Even if it's for a day or a weekend, the Bruce Trail is a gem to be savored.

Geology of the Niagara Escarpment

$\mathcal{M}$ost of us recognize the escarpment's most notable formation, Niagara Falls. But the escarpment extends far beyond this magnificent sight. It actually begins east of Rochester, New York, near Union Hill, and stretches to Wisconsin. Along the way, it sometimes disappears into farmland or sinks beneath lakes.

Four geological formations contributed to the making of today's escarpment. The first began approximately 430 million years ago, during the geological period called Upper Ordovician. At that time, the Appalachian Mountains on the eastern coast of the U.S. were as high as the Rocky Mountains. As these mountains eroded, ancient rivers carried the sediment westward into a delta region where Lake Ontario and Lake Erie exist today. This sediment hardened into red shale and sandstone forming the escarpment's base.

The second formation that contributed to the escarpment was a giant shallow sea that lay in a depression of the earth's crust, the center of which is located in the state of Michigan. The sea slowly filled and flooded the river delta region. Over millions of years the ocean's plant and animal life died, mixing with ocean minerals. Over time, the ocean waters rose and fell depositing varying types and amounts of sediment into distinct layers, such as soft shale, sandstone, limestone, and dolostone.

Then the third geological change came about. Changes in the earth's crust caused the Michigan Basin to rise, slowly draining the waters. Over millions of years, erosion began removing the softer shale underlying the more resistant dolostone. As the softer material eroded away, large chunks of dolostone broke off creating cliffs. Today, erosion continues to be the most important factor shaping the escarpment. Water and wave action have created dramatic results, such as cliffs along the shores of Georgian Bay on the Bruce Peninsula.

The fourth and last change occurred in the most recent of geologic times. At least four glaciers buried the area in sheets of ice one to two miles (2 to 3 km) thick. Each glacier left its mark by widening valleys, scraping rock layers off the top of the escarpment, and depositing mounds of rock below the cliffs. The last glacier, known as the Wisconsin, retreated 12,000 years ago.

World Biosphere Reserve

What do the Everglades, the Serengeti Desert, and the Galapagos Islands have in common with the Niagara Escarpment? They are all classified as Biosphere Reserves by the United Nations Educational, Scientific, and Cultural Organization (UNESCO). The Niagara Escarpment joined this prestigious group on February 8, 1990, based on nominations submitted by more than ten countries.

UNESCO conceived of the "Man and the Biosphere" program some 20 years ago. This program led to the formal recognition of the Biosphere Reserve concept. A Biosphere Reserve is an area that has successfully balanced conservation and preservation of a significant ecosystem with surrounding development. It recognizes that humans must coexist with nature and the natural environment.

A Biosphere Reserve has three key areas: a core area which is minimally disturbed, a buffer zone which allows activities compatible with the conservation of the core area, and the transitional zone where sustainable resource use and management is encouraged in cooperation with the people who live in the area.

The Niagara Escarpment Commission and Parks Canada have systems in place to protect and preserve the unique flora and fauna found on the Niagara Escarpment. The Niagara Escarpment Planning and Development Act established the Niagara Escarpment Plan in 1985, making this one of the few world biosphere reserves to be protected by legislation

Bruce Trail Association

*E*ach brilliant idea needs someone of courage and stamina to dream it and bring it to fruition. The Bruce Trail was the brainchild of Raymond Lowes, a member of the Hamilton Naturalist Club conservation committee. It was his dream to create a hiking trail along the entire 451-mile (726 km) route of the Niagara Escarpment.

In 1960, a Bruce Trail committee was formed consisting of Norman Pearson (chairman), Raymond Lowes (secretary), Philip Gosling, and Robert MacLaren. The committee received a grant from the Atkinson Foundation, and in 1963, the Bruce Trail Association was incorporated. After seven years of exhaustive work, the Bruce Trail officially opened in 1967 on Canada's centennial.

Today, the Bruce Trail Association has 8,000 members and 800 active volunteers supporting nine volunteer clubs, each responsible for a segment of the trail. Thirty percent of the Bruce Trail is on private land. So, in addition to trail development and maintenance, landowner relations is a major function of the Bruce Trail Association.

Signs and blazes common along the Bruce Trail.

Bruce Trail
(Southern Half)

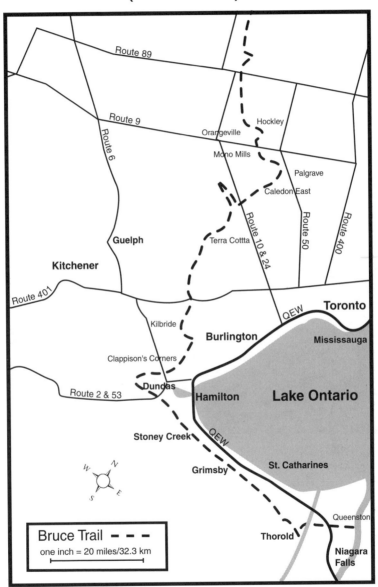

Route 89

Route 9

Route 6

Hockley

Orangeville

Mono Mills

Palgrave

Caledon East

Route 10 & 24

Route 50

Route 400

Guelph

Terra Cottta

Kitchener

Route 401

Kilbride

Burlington

QEW

Toronto

Mississauga

Clappison's Corners

Route 2 & 53

Dundas

Hamilton

Lake Ontario

Stoney Creek

QEW

N
W   E
S

Grimsby

St. Catharines

Queenston

Thorold

Niagara
Falls

Bruce Trail - - -
one inch = 20 miles/32.3 km

Our Journal

Off to a good start! Rich and Sue in front of the General
Brock Memorial in Queenston Heights.

A Slow Start

August 13, Day 1

It was a beautiful day to begin a hike. Of course, any day is a good day to begin a hike. Yesterday we had a leisurely drive from Rochester, New York, to our cousins' house in Stoney Creek, Ontario. Thanks to their kindness, we would use their house as a base to begin and end our journey.

After breakfast, Cathy and Ray drove us from Stoney Creek to the trailhead in Queenston Heights. We were excited to get underway, to explore the unknown that lay ahead, to once again experience the freedom of a long backpacking trip. We had trouble finding the start of the Bruce Trail and had to ask several people. Finally, we picked up the white blazes but never did see the cairn. So be it. We wanted to get moving. We hugged the cousins goodbye and started off into the woods. After five minutes, we doubled back and took a compass reading, afraid we were on another trail called the General Brock Trail. But finally we decided we were OK and proceeded.

Switchbacks took us part of the way down the escarpment to an abandoned railroad bed. City noises from cars on the QEW and trains passing by surrounded us. It rained last night so the woods were damp, and the mosquitoes were voracious. We caught periodic views of the valley below, but a heavy fog limited visibility. I wished we knew about the geology of the area. Signs pointed out interesting places with line drawings of what we were seeing, but they didn't describe what it was. The packs felt heavy; they were not our friends yet! And we were out of shape. Rich was grumbling and low on commitment, but he knew that even though this was a short trip, he wouldn't make it if he wasn't totally committed. Thank goodness for the overcast skies to keep off the sun. Even so, we were warm. Or were we just out of shape? The thermometer said 71° F (22° C). So far the Bruce Trail was pretty easy—a nice dirt footbed, mostly flat with some short but steep ups-and-downs. It's

Sue approaching the pond at Fireman's Park.

well blazed, and we appreciated the offset double blazes in this section telling us the direction to turn.

We stopped for lunch on a grassy knoll overlooking a pond in Fireman's Park. The slight breeze kept the bugs at bay. It was slow going today, not due to the Bruce Trail, but due to us. We were waiting for inspiration, and our bodies were stiff from lack of physical activity. The first rule of long-distance hiking is to begin slowly, hiking six to eight miles for the first few days. This allows for two things. First, the body needs to gradually build endurance. A warm-up period of a few days to a week will pay dividends further down the trail with fewer pulled or strained muscles. The second reason for beginning slowly involves the feet. They aren't used to walking many miles at a time, especially with the additional weight of a pack. Taking it slowly reduces the chances of stress fractures and, hopefully, results in fewer blisters.

We knew this part of the trail would be busy. So far we'd encountered three day hikers with dogs, three kids on bikes, and one kid fishing at a pond. The noises of civilization intruded—gravel pit machinery, lawn mowers, golf course yells, cars, and trains. It was like exploring the back lots as a kid. Shortly after Fireman's Park, the trail became distinctly more hilly, much more like the Appalachian Trail in Georgia, then a long road walk. Road walks were a double-edged sword. They got us out of the wooded green tunnel to see horses, farms, gardens, and vineyards, but the pavement was tough on our feet.

The Bruce Trail paralleled the abandoned third Welland

Canal in a long narrow corridor beside the old stone locks. The gates and machinery have been removed, and the water now cascades through the series of former locks in waterfall fashion. The cacophony of falling water drowned out the city noises. An interesting part of history most people in cars never see.

Welland Canal

The Welland Canal, which carries ships down 326.5 feet (99.5 m) from Lake Erie to Lake Ontario, is actually the fourth in a series of canals built through this narrow strip of land to circumvent Niagara Falls. The first Welland Canal was opened in 1829. It was widened, deepened, and rerouted over the

The abandoned third Welland Canal.

years. The third canal was in use from 1887 to 1931. The current canal opened in 1932 but was rerouted out of downtown Welland in 1973. Today's canal has seven locks which operate by gravity. It takes about 12 hours for a laker or ocean-going vessel to travel from lake to lake through the locks. The bridge that the Bruce Trail crosses on Glendale Avenue is a vertical lift bridge, which rises 120 feet (36.6 m) to allow the passage of ships. As you cross the Glendale Avenue bridge and turn south along the Welland Canal, you are looking toward lock number 4. Locks 4, 5, and 6 are called the twin-flight locks. This refers to the side-by-side locks at each level allowing two-way traffic through the three consecutive locks.

By 3:30 p.m. we found a place to camp. Our first day out was short, but don't tell that to our sore and tired bodies. I had swollen ankles and hips, and shoulders sore with heat rash. Rich said the bottoms of his feet hurt, and his legs felt like they weighed a ton. It's a slow job getting these old bodies in gear again. We found a way down to the water next to some boulders, stepping carefully so as not to slip and be carried away through the locks. Using bandannas, we washed up in the raging canal waters and felt immensely better. We were glad to have a green tent. It's much less visible in the woods, and we felt safer in these populated areas. Dinner consisted of macaroni and cheese, peas, and a cup of hot lime Jell-O® gelatin. Neither of us was very hungry, just tired. By 4:30 p.m. a steady sprinkle drove us quickly into the tent.

By 5:30 p.m. I was sound asleep. I don't know if it was the hiking or Rich's reading to me that made me sleepy. We brought two things for entertainment, a paperback book and a Walkman® radio. Each night we planned to read aloud. The book, *Paddle To The Arctic*, was an autobiography about a kayaker attempting to be the first to cross the Arctic Circle. It made us realize that we had things pretty easy compared to the hardships faced by this fellow! If he could paddle the arctic seas, we could surely continue hiking. An hour later, I awoke to find the skies had cleared, so we took advantage of it to exit our tent, go to the bathroom, and brush our teeth.

Canal Hopping
August 14, Day 2

Woke up at 7 a.m. after 14 hours of sleep. Not bad proportions, 6 hours of hiking to 14 hours of sleep. Broke camp by 8:15 a.m. and enjoyed the Welland Canal. We backtracked a lot this morning; because we neglected to follow the blazes very closely. At one point, a ship in the canal distracted us, and we went straight ahead while the trail turned right. At other times, many intersecting trails crisscrossed, and we chose the wrong one. We arrived at Glendale Avenue by 9:30 a.m. passing two grocery stores, a McDonald's, and a Burger King. We even passed a nice breakfast restaurant. In a few weeks, we would probably stop even if we had just finished breakfast. But our hiker appetites weren't fully developed yet. However, when we came upon a Tim Horton's store, famous for coffee and donuts, Rich couldn't resist stopping.

Most of the woods we walked through were very young forests. We ate lunch in the shady grass while our socks, shirts, and packs dried in a sunny spot nearby. We had hoped to take a dip in Lake Moodie, but the current was fierce and signs stated "no swimming," so we settled at DeCew House Park to rest and fuel our bodies. Rich broke out the moleskin to cover parts of his feet. I felt better today, since I found some pull tabs on my pack that I had forgot-

Walking along the current Welland Canal with the
Glendale Avenue liftbridge in the background.

A short walk along an abandoned railroad.

The trail takes us into an abandoned lock
from the old Welland Canal.

ten about. After cinching them down, my pack rode much more comfortably. Kudos to the trail maintainers throughout this section. They dug trenches along the trail in the clay and used it to raise the trail bed. That's a lot of work! Obviously this is a wet area part of the year—not this August though. The ground was parched and cracked, and creek beds were bone dry.

This trail was proving to be packed with variety. We wandered through wooded trails for a while, sauntered by housing tracts, passed commercial areas, relived days of canals past, and savored views of the valley below the escarpment. Each half hour brought something different. At first Rich didn't like all the commerce and civilization along the trail, but it added a different type of experience. It's all in your point of view. We did miss the camaraderie of having a few hikers around. We have seen only a few day hikers so far, and the people at Tim Horton's looked at us like we were from the moon. Maybe it was just our smell. We took a long break at lunch, lying lazily in the grass watching the martins diving toward the water catching bugs in midair. A sundog streaked across the sky for our enjoyment. This was living. The walk around Moodie Lake was sunny and pleasant. Midway we broke out our sun hats. The trail wound around and took us along the top of a tall stone dike. Near the end, we followed the escarpment edge with a sharp drop off and periodic views of the Niagara Valley and Lake Ontario. We filled up with water from the spigot at Morningstar Mill, a wonderful old mill that has been restored and sits atop DeCew Falls. Sticking our heads out the mill window, we had the best view of the falls . The water ran to the edge of a hanging rock slab and fell freely to the shady valley below.

Rich walks along the dike above Lake Moodie.

Morningstar Mill

Morningstar Mill was built next to DeCew Falls in 1872 by Robert Chappel using limestone from the creek that feeds the mill. Water from the creek ran through a turbine at the bottom of a 40-foot deep pit inside the mill. This was one of the first mills in Canada run by a turbine rather than a waterwheel.

Wilson Morningstar purchased the mill in 1883 and turned it into a community hub. The land around DeCew Falls contained a sawmill, gristmill, blacksmith shop, carpentry shop, cider mill, community hall for dances, and a shoddy mill. Shoddy was a fabric made from reclaimed wool used in the upholstery of cheap furniture. For gristmill services, Morningstar kept 1/12 of the flour or feed produced. For each 60 lbs. (27 kg) of wheat a farmer brought to the mill, 42 lbs. (19 kg) of flour and 18 lbs. (8 kg) of byproduct were produced.

After a fire in 1895 destroyed everything but the stone structure, Wilson Morningstar rebuilt the gristmill. He designed and built innovative equipment for sifting, oat flaking, and purifying wheat. This equipment remains on the site today.

In 1933 Mr. Morningstar died, and his relatives operated the mill for a few years, then sold it to Ontario Hydro. In 1982 the city of St. Catharines bought the mill but didn't have the money to renovate it. Volunteers came to the rescue. In 1992 a group of concerned citi-

Morningstar Mill

zens took on the task and formed the "Friends of Morningstar Mill." Over 30 people have contributed to the restoration project. They rebuilt the old machinery which had sat idle for 60 years. Today the mill once again runs on water power and retains its original character. The "Friends" are also restoring the Morningstars' 1898 five-bedroom Victorian home. When completed, it will serve as an interpretive center.

The view of DeCew Falls from inside Morningstar Mill.

After a short road walk, we headed into the woods and escaped the city noises for the first time. We camped far back in the woods just past the only flowing creek we could find. We've been surprised by the people we've met and passed along the way. Rarely were they friendly, not making eye contact or returning our hello. That was too bad. We may look scuzzy, but we are really very nice. People sometimes judge others too quickly by outward appearance.

We were purposely keeping our daily hiking distance short to break in our bodies slowly. Although we were both sore in various places, our endurance was better today. On the trail at 8 a.m., we didn't bed down until 6:30 p.m., a much longer day. I read to Rich tonight, but only for 30 minutes before he asked to go to sleep.

Any Port in the Storm
August 15, Day 3

Crossed two gravel roads, then hiked up a steep hill to the grass-covered escarpment with views back over hills to the east. The long grassy summit reminded us of the southern mountain balds in Virginia. We were glad for the cloud cover to shield us from the sun. We entered the mature woods of Short Hills and watched three young raccoons scurry up the trees next to the trail. Last night and again this morning as we packed up, a buck deer snorted at us. We were on his turf, and he was not at all happy.

Since we began, stream beds have been dry, except the large ones like Twelve Mile Creek, and there have been no springs. So we had to take water from small lakes and ponds when possible. The water was cloudy from dolomite dust and tasted different from what were used to. We filtered it through a bandanna to eliminate the large sediment and treated it with iodine tablets to kill any microscopic organisms.

The Bruce Trail proved that it wasn't a wimp today. The first two days broke us in easy with gentle terrain and clay paths. Today we broke a sweat as we pounded up and down gullies carved deep into the escarpment through erosion. The easy clay path turned to talus and boulder fields. Our leg muscles began to burn, partly from the steep terrain and partly from the thorns and sharp-edged plant leaves that cut us. There wasn't a switchback in sight. Today's trail sorely needed a trim job. We ducked under and around branches. Our legs and feet were slapped by tall weeds and grasses that if wet would have soaked our shorts and drenched our legs, dripping into our boots. Thank goodness the vegetation was dry today. But, the dryness also meant that all of the creek beds were dry. In spring, this trail must be loaded with pretty waterfalls as water cascades over the rock ledges in the creek beds. It was a hot and tiring afternoon— a fun hike in the woods, with some good climbs and lots of dry waterfalls. The barometer on Rich's watch (a "guy toy") showed that the pressure was dropping, and we felt the wind shifting to the south. It was going to rain. We stopped to talk with two women hikers who said that this was a rough section. It sure felt rough to our still out-of-shape bodies.

We kept seeing and hearing Canada geese. Today on a road walk we passed a small, low-water, quarry pond. As we sat along the road eating lunch, we watched a flock of geese fly by, circle back, and land on the pond. They were desperate for water too.

We reached Balls Falls (a misnomer today since there was no water over the falls) and stopped to use the restroom and fill up with water. While on our pit stop, it began to rain. We took refuge under a pavilion and waited it out while debating our options. They were: hike on and get wet, call a bed-and-breakfast, or camp under the park pavilion and risk getting kicked out. Rich was in favor of the B&B, I preferred to stay and risk getting kicked out. We decided to cook dinner in the pavilion and postpone our decision. It was only 4 p.m. and we had eaten a late lunch, so neither of us was very hungry. While Rich cooked, I read aloud from the book. After dinner we cleaned up, brushed our teeth, and tried to stay warm. The storm was brought on by a passing cold front. We hunched together on a picnic bench, wearing both our rain jackets and fleece jackets. Then by 6:30 p.m., the sky cleared and the temperature rose. A wedding was being readied in the chapel near the pavilion, so we decided to hike on. We hiked for an hour before finding a suitable tent site.

Rich is fussy about finding just the right tent site. It has to be relatively flat but absolutely not visible from the trail. So, we traipsed along the trail farther than I'd prefer. It was 8 p.m. and getting dark by the time we settled in. The rain did some good—we saw a trickle of a waterfall in the first stream we crossed. It was a good day, and I was tired and ready for sleep. I got my first blister today, on my little toe.

At 9 p.m. a bolt of lightning streaked across the sky and a crack of thunder peeled through the air. The sky opened and dumped a wall of water. It rained most of the night, but we stayed dry in our nest. A quarry operation somewhere in the distance droned on with machinery noises and the beep, beep of vehicles backing. Though the noise lasted most of the night and started again at daybreak, at one point I awoke to silence except for the horse whinny of a screech owl.

Where'd the Trail Go?
August 16, Day 4

Too noisy to sleep so we got up at 6 a.m. The morning was hot and humid. We walked a long way at the base of the escarpment, dripping in sweat. The wet leaves felt good against our legs. Eventually, we climbed the escarpment and found a welcome breeze. We ran out of water, and my journal writing pen ran out of ink. Finally at a road crossing, we found a house where a young man willingly gave us cold fresh Brita® water and even offered us a new pen.

The trail fooled me again. I was leading the way, and after a few climbs through dry creek beds, the path turned into the ideal dream of a level, narrow, mowed grass path with shade trees overhead and a strong breeze blowing. My mind wandered and I picked up the pace, enjoying the easy trail. After about ten minutes I said to Rich, "Have you seen a blaze lately?" He said, "No, I was daydreaming," mean - ing, "No, you were in the lead; it was your responsibility to watch the blazes." So, we backtracked and found that short- ly after the idyllic trail started, the Bruce Trail veered to the right. We took the Bruce Trail this time, climbing up and down over wet, slippery escarpment rocks that looked like meteorite stones with their water-carved pock marks. The trail wound around and even crossed the idyllic path later on.

Pock Marks

Pitting and pock marks in the escarpment rock were formed by chemical weathering of the carbonate rocks. Rain water plus carbon dioxide combine to form carbonic acid that eats away at the rocks. Algae, lichen, and mosses which grow on the rocks form organic acids also.

Eventually, we reached the public pool at Kinsman Park. It wasn't open for 45 minutes, but the teenager cleaning it let us use the showers. After the heat and sweat of the morning's hike, the frigid cold shower was refreshing. We spread our stuff, including the wet tent, in the wind to dry. The sky had clouded over, and it looked like it would rain again. When the pool opened we went in for a quick swim. We hadn't intended it to be quick, but the water was as frigid as the showers, so we didn't dally. We ate a leisurely lunch at a picnic table while we wore our wet clothes, hoping that they would dry out. No such luck. There was no sun and high humidity, so even the wind didn't help. Rich had made the mistake of washing his socks. Now he had to hike all afternoon in wet socks. But he was happy that at least they were clean.

If you're ever looking for a fun hike for just the day along the Bruce Trail, we recommend the section in the Mountainview Conservation Area between Mountainview Road and Thirty Mountain Road. It's a rock jungle that gives you a feel for escarpment rocks and cliffs, up close and personal. The area is lush with vivid green vegetation even in August. Many of the rocks are moss covered. We found it very slippery as weeks of clay dust were wetted by last night's rain. It was a slow-going section. We didn't change a lot in real elevation, but found ourselves going up and down continually. A good aerobic workout and picturesque too.

Lush greens cover the escarpment rocks in
Mountainview Conservation Area.

We had to stop at a house to fill water bottles for tonight's dinner and tomorrow's breakfast. Closer to Lake Ontario today, we had good views of the crisp blue water. So close and yet so far away. As we filled our water bottles, we saw a thunderhead form over the lake. Then loud thunder peeled in the distance. Later, as we cooked dinner, the thunder stopped and the wind died down. We thought perhaps we would be spared. Not so. By 6 p.m. we were snug in the tent. Within a minute it started to rain. We had timed it perfectly once again. It was so hot inside the tent, we were hoping the rain would cool things off. Read aloud for a while then fell asleep.

Pit Stop Number One
August 17, Day 5

$\mathcal{R}$ich tried to roust me at 6:30 a.m. after 11 hours of sleep, but I didn't want to move. Not only was it still raining lightly, but I could hear an owl hooting not far away. So if the owl thought it was still night, I could too. Finally, Rich won out and we got going. I underestimated the Bruce. I thought, since there are no mountain ranges, how hard could following the escarpment be? But it was tough. Lots of climbs. We noticed this morning that even though the trails went straight up and down, there was no erosion problem and no water bars. I guess the water chooses the many deep escarpment chasms and rolls off the hard-packed clay of the trails. The clay was slippery this morning from the night's rain. By 8:30 a.m. I had already fallen on my butt once.

We had a long boring road walk along Ridge Road and Woolverton Mountain Road. We were close to Lake Ontario and could see the Toronto skyline across the water. Off in the distance, a laker was cutting through the blue water heading toward the Welland Canal. Just as we entered the woods, the sky opened with a brief, light shower. Once again, the heavy tree canopy protected us from getting wet. The next section of trail was a long traverse across the face of the escarpment. The going was tough due to the high vegetation, which obscured our view in a section where we needed to place each foot carefully. We came to a recent landslide and had to climb over downed trees and across slicks of loose clay. For miles we battled through "prolific plant." At the time, I didn't know its real name, but it grew everywhere so we dubbed it "prolific plant." Some plants were ankle high and some head high, but most, waist to shoulder high. It had teardrop shaped, serrated leaves, a round stalk, and a small yellow snapdragon flower. Thankfully, prolific plant was soft to the touch, unlike the nettle patches we sometimes trudged through. I felt like Dorothy, in the movie *The Wizard Of Oz*, as she ran through the poppy field.

Touch-me-not

Our prolific plant turned out to be touch-me-not, also called jewelweed, a soft succulent herb with pale translucent stems. The annuals impatiens are part of the touch-me-not family.

We saw both genera of touch-me-not in great profusion along the Bruce Trail. The spotted touch-me-not (impatiens capensis) had golden orange flowers often splotched with reddish brown. The pale touch-me-not had larger pale yellow flowers with only occasional brown spots. The name touch-me-not derives from the fruit of the plant, which is a swollen capsule that explodes when touched, expelling its seeds.

It is also a proven, highly effective antidote for poison ivy. By rubbing the juice of crushed leaves and stems on the skin immediately after exposure, the poison ivy's oil is neutralized.

Waist deep in Touch-me-nots.

Yellow Clintonia

It was the bright blue berries that caught our eye. By fall, the draught of summer had yellowed the leaves, but the blue berries were a stark contrast to the greens and yellows of the forest floor. Also commonly called bluebead lily, it has a feathery yellow flower from May through August. The berries are somewhat poisonous and should not be confused with blueberries.

For some of the trail, the maintainers had actually moved rocks off to the side—how wonderful! The section after 50 Road was fairly level and well trimmed, so we trucked along at a rapid rate. Rich actually asked for a break, which was a change of roles. He's more a morning person, and I'm more an afternoon person.

Civilization closed back in on us as we approached Stoney Creek. The trail became a narrow corridor between backyards at the bottom of the escarpment (many with inviting swimming pools) and roads at the top of the escarpment. We continued traversing on fairly level ground and made good time. But, by the time we approached the house of my cousins, Cathy and Ray, we had put in a long day and our feet and legs hurt. As we approached their house, it began to sprinkle. Once again we were in shelter, warm and dry, as the rain hit. My cousins welcomed us with gracious hospitality including a shower, home-cooked meal, laundry, and warm dry bed. It felt so good, and we sure smelled a lot better afterward.

The Green Corridor
August 18, Day 6

Slept in this morning and took Cathy and Ray out for a hearty breakfast. I left most of our mail drop food at Cathy and Ray's. Our hiker appetites hadn't kicked in yet. Still, both of us polished off big dinners last night and breakfasts this morning. Maybe it's just trail food that's unappetizing. Shortly after leaving Stoney Creek, we climbed to the top of the mountain (as the locals call it) and followed the trail along the top edge with a nice breeze blowing on this warm and sunny day. The trail along the top was what we had envisioned the Bruce Trail to be like—a fairly flat, dirt path. It was great; we hoped this section would last a long time. We passed Felker's Falls and actually saw water cascading over the rocks—our first waterfall with water since the canal area. Yeah! The streams were running in this section, although the water looked rather murky. We learned from Cathy and Ray that the storm we heard over Lake Ontario a few days ago included a tornado that touched down near Dundas, lifting houses off their foundations. It looked like it dumped enough rain so that we would have water for a while. Cathy had given us each a tangerine, and we munched them for our morning break along a gurgling stream. Ahhh, sweet nectar. Rich put moleskin on the balls of his feet, sore from the pounding. My toes were very cramped. My feet swell as I hike, so boots that feel fine when I first put them on, soon are too small.

We headed down the escarpment then back up and picked up a paved railroad bed ten miles (16.1 km) long, which led us ever so gradually toward Hamilton. The walk was easy but the pavement was hard on the soles of our feet. Wide-brimmed hats shielded our faces from the scorching sun. We were surprised by how heavily used this hikeway/bikeway was for a Monday mid-day. The views were spectacular—the sprawl of Hamilton, the curve of the escarpment, and the Toronto skyline off in the distance. We even came upon a brick-making factory in action as we descended.

All morning, we were overwhelmed by the strong laundry-detergent smell of our clothes. We only used half a cup of liquid detergent in the washer and nothing in the dryer, but our noses weren't used to the strong perfume smell.

Rich said his pack was beginning to become his friend. He was finally relaxing and not in a rush today. I've felt that way since day one. Walking in the woods is my favorite way to soothe mind and body.

The Bruce Trail veered off the bike path and headed up the escarpment. We crossed over a highway bridge just above the city of Hamilton. The escarpment here is 195 feet (59 m) high and posed a significant barrier to the early settlers of Hamilton. Our trek through Hamilton was a delightful surprise. On the map it looked like a long stretch through city neighborhoods. But the trail builders did a wonderful job of keeping the Bruce Trail in a green corridor, only coming out to cross major bridges which had the advantage

Hamilton comes into view at the base of the escarpment,
with Lake Ontario in the distance.

A brick-making factory at the base of the escarpment
in Hamilton.

of rewarding us with glorious views down into Hamilton. The people here, were active, outdoors people and friendly too. Hamilton is crossed with bike routes and hiking trails, and we passed many people of all ages out enjoying the trail network. We've decided that people who are outdoors exercising in some way are friendlier. They greeted us with smiles and waves.

Again in need of water, We found someone home at the fourth house we tried. A young woman with two small children filled our water bottles and added ice cubes with rose petals frozen inside. She explained that they were left over from a party. Nothing like elegant hiking with rose-petal water!

Pausing for a drink, Rich crosses a highway bridge over downtown Hamilton.

We did another good long day today and nested in the woods near Iroquoia Heights Conservation Area. The end of today's walk was a wonderful stroll up a long and gradual old road now converted to a bike path with a cinder bed. We needed the slow walk because we had stopped at the Chedoke Golf Club snack bar and had cheeseburgers, french fries, cole slaw, and cola for dinner. Both of us felt full, heavy, and queasy. The golf club was an interesting use of land. It had the typical golf course plus a hiking and biking trail through the center of it and a ski resort on top of it. In winter, the trail is closed and the skiers use the greens and fairways. Great idea and an exceptional use of land!

I was worried about my little toes. They hurt today, and at the end of the day, I unwrapped them and found they'd both grown some nasty looking blisters. I drained the blisters, covered them with NewSkin®, and rebandaged them with toilet paper held on with white adhesive tape. I hoped I could get my boots on. The radio said we were in for three days of nice weather.

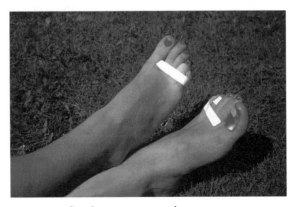

Sue's uncooperative toes.

Life is a series
of choices.
Choose wisely.

Splish Splash

August 19, Day 7

*R*ich rousted me grudgingly awake again this morning. Both of us found it difficult to choke down our cold Pop Tarts® toaster pastries. We began the day by hiking over rugged terrain with climbs and lots of rocks, then we took our morning candy bar break at Sherman Falls. By 10 a.m. my toes hurt already. We cut away my lower insoles, and I wore only the outer socks in an attempt to give my toes more room.

We came upon a young couple camped at the falls. With a quick glance, we could see that they were beginning campers. She was wearing a cotton sweatshirt. Their tent was set-up in the middle of the trail, near a busy road, and next to a noisy waterfall—not the safest place to camp. He was busy building a fire to make coffee in a large coffee pot. A few minutes ago, he was putting on deodorant. It looked like they had lots of heavy gear.

We climbed the escarpment above Sherman Falls and walked into hiker heaven—mile after wonderful mile of the Dundas Valley System with wide, graded, dirt paths. My toes were so grateful. We stopped at the trail center to fill up on water and use the restrooms, but the concession stand was closed. Drats!

Sherman Falls

Rich says wonderment set in for him on day six. Instead of focusing just on the trail, he now looked at everything. I wonder what is around the next bend? I wonder what kind of bird that is? I wonder what kind of flower that is? All of a sudden he had a childlike curiosity.

The groomed trails eventually ended, but the terrain remained mild. We paralleled the train tracks and watched two trains—a Canadian National freight train and a VIA passenger train—pass quickly above us. Then it was on past Dundas Golf and Country Club, up the escarpment and then back down, and ending at the base of Webster Falls. Lots of people were playing in the water, so we joined them on this warm, sunny afternoon. We stood below the 150-foot (46 m) drop and let the cool water pummel us. I sat in

The top of Webster Falls with an arched stone
bridge over the creek.

Rich being pummeled at the base of Webster Falls.

narrow channels as the water rushed through. The water felt almost warm. We washed off all the sweat and grime and cooled our bodies as we played. With our fill of watery playtime, we headed up the escarpment and marched over to view Tews Falls. This falls was just as high as Webster Falls, but the water had a straight shot from a cantilevered rim all the way to the bottom.

The afternoon ended with a long, slow road walk along Fallsview Road East. Just as we were beginning to think it wouldn't end, a mirage appeared. But it was real after all. On the corner of Fallsview Road East and Sydenham Road sat a beautiful farm market selling fruits, vegetables, pies, breads, and even ice cream with a choice of fresh fruit blended in. And, they welcomed hikers. I had ice cream with fresh raspberries in a sugar cone. Rich had his ice cream with peaches. Those polished off, we dug into raspberry and apple turnovers. Then we bought a cucumber, a tomato, and four ears of corn to go. Add four bottles of water and we left the mirage with heavy loads but with smiles on our faces. When we made camp near Rock Chapel, we continued our feast. Best trail food we'd had yet, but it didn't do much to reduce the weight of our food bag.

My toes seemed to be doing fairly well, at least no worse. We babied them today by taking frequent breaks. Each time we stopped, I'd take my boots off to dry my socks and air my feet. Happy toes mean a happy hiker.

Trail Magic
August 20, Day 8

The night's sleep was good; Rich enjoyed listening to trains rumble in the valley below. Sometime in the night, an animal stood nearby and gave a raspy growl that had the same rhythm as a cat purring. For the last few days the weather had been nice, cool and breezy, but now it looked like rain might be here by tonight.

We encountered rougher terrain this morning with climbs and rocks. I wasn't awake, walking along in a daze, trying to keep my balance. Rich as usual bounded ahead. We reversed roles in the afternoon.

We came to a sign saying that the next 200 meters (656 ft) was under surveillance and was not being maintained at the request of the landowner. Most of the trail so far seemed unmaintained, at least in the matter of foliage control. Crossing Highway 6 was a death-defying experience. We had to cross four lanes of traffic rushing to work, including lots of tractor-trailer trucks. They even had the downhill advantage on us. We waited a long while and timed our mad dash very carefully. We must have looked funny with our packs bouncing along.

The black clay of Stoney Creek gave way to a nice brown loam. The trail became a wander in the woods, up and down the hills through a middle-aged oak, maple, and ash forest. We were surrounded now by the sounds of the forest. This section had wide dirt paths and nice bridges. A breeze- and cloud-filled sky kept us cool. Once again, the Bruce Trail showed us its variety.

Rich's wonderment turned into thankfulness. Everything he saw, heard, smelled, or touched, he silently gave thanks for. In Rich's words, "All of it combined makes a perfect place. Being on the trail our senses are slowly opening, revealing the perfect order of it all." He's getting philosophical on me.

We followed a stream (with water) through a valley then climbed beside it as it cascaded through a cut in the escarpment. We continued climbing up through a field then finally leveled out. On a grassy path parallel to Mt. Brow Road, we stopped for lunch. The white medical tape on my foot itched, and scratching it, I burst a blister. Unknown to me, blisters had formed on the tops of both feet at the base of my toes under the tape. In trying to fix one problem, I created another. I brushed the toes with NewSkin® to cover these new wounds. My feet have become quite a sight. Rich, on the other hand, was feeling smug. He said his boots felt like slippers.

I was trudging along thinking how badly my feet hurt, when right in front of us on the trail was trail magic! Two unopened bottles of Coronas Extra® beer. It took Rich a few minutes, but he managed to open the bottles on a tree stump. We were next to the Burlington Quarry, so we sat on a stone ledge overlooking Hamilton and Lake Ontario. Having now seen almost every angle of Hamilton, we

Trail magic! Sue sits on the edge of the Burlington
Quarry enjoying a free beer.

Sue carefully descending after the beer.

toasted her with our beer and, in absentia, thanked the trail angel. Warm beer goes down real easy on a cool day.

On our way again, the trail immediately dropped down a rock cliff. As was inevitable, we soon climbed back up, this time to the top of a grass-covered hill that gave us views of the Toronto skyline once again. Crossing Highway 5 was almost as difficult as crossing Highway 6 had been. We got a break with a lull in the cars and dashed across. But, our luck ran out as we walked along Highway 5, and it started to rain. Strong winds drove the rain straight into our bellies, drenching us quickly. We took refuge in a garden center, which, by the way, had nice restrooms. Rich listened to the weather forecast on the radio. Several days of rain were expected, so we decided to make the best of it. The Terra Garden Store employees let us use their phone to call the only two motels in Waterdown. The Artesian was full, but the Waterdown Motel had a room. The kindly owner of Terra let one of his employees drive us to the motel in his truck. So, ten minutes later we were at Waterdown Motel. The owner came out, took one look at us, and said, "No rooms available!" I think he decided we were vagrants. It wasn't fun being discriminated against, especially when we were cold, wet, and tired.

Now, without a ride, we walked back toward Waterdown, again into the oncoming rain and wind, and stopped at the first establishment—a Tim Horton's. At least some warm soup would help. I pulled out my list of possible lodgings and found two more motels back at Clappison's Corners. Rich used the outside phone to call the Escarpment View Motel. Not only did they have an opening, but they were

offering a special rate because they were undergoing reno-
vations. I asked Rich to reserve the room using a credit card.
They didn't take credit cards but assured us that they would
hold the room for one hour, the time it would take us to
walk the 2.5 miles (4 km). Rich made sure they knew that
we were hiking the Bruce Trail. So with warm, full bellies,
and refuge in mind, we headed west on Highway 5, away
from the trail. This time the wind was at our backs, and with
rainjackets, hats, gaiters, and packcovers all tightly clasped
around us, we were much warmer even though we were
walking in the pounding rain. Each large truck that passed
sprayed us sideways. It felt like being in a dishwasher.

The people at the Escarpment View Motel were true to
their word and rented us a room. Within minutes we shed
our wet stuff, took hot showers, and collapsed on the bed. It
felt wonderful to be warm, dry, and clean. The weather forecast on TV looked grim. Several days of rain and cold were
in store.

$\mathcal{A}$ $\mathcal{D}ay$ Off
$\mathcal{A}ugust$ $21,$ $\mathcal{D}ay$ 9

$\mathcal{W}$e intended to sleep in this morning but actually woke at our usual time—6:30 a.m. We lounged in bed dozing on and off while watching *Good Morning America* on TV. We decided to take a day off the trail and relax. The temperature outside was in the 50s (10°C) with a high forecast in the mid 60s (18°C). It had rained hard overnight and was still drizzling with intermittent rain expected. Outside, the world was shrouded in a dense fog. Not exactly the best day to climb Mt. Nemo. Besides, my feet needed a day of rest to give the blisters a chance to heal. When I unwrapped the bandages last night, I found two more blisters. Around 9:30 a.m. we straggled out of bed and took showers. I doused my blisters with NewSkin® and let them dry thoroughly. We dressed in long pants, long-sleeved shirts, raincoats, hats, and sandals, and shuffled back up Highway 5 for half a mile (0.8 km) to a restaurant. We still had plenty of trail food with us, but a real meal only half a mile away was just too appealing to pass up. There wasn't much else to see or do at Clappison's Corners, so we bought a *USA Today* newspaper and brought it back to our motel room. After a few hours of gazing through the windows at the rain, we began to think about life.

Rich's thoughts on a rainy day: Yesterday as we walked, I

thought of all that I was thankful for. Many times I worry about things. Sue, on the other hand, doesn't seem to worry about anything. Between the two of us, we worry an average amount. This time, I told myself that I wasn't going to worry about the impending bad weather or what we would do. Instead I talked to "Judy," my guardian angel. All right I know it sounds funny, both that I talk to one and that I call her by name. Plus, it sure isn't a macho thing, so I don't tell anyone. Anyway, I wasn't going to worry, and I told Judy that I would flow with whatever was best for us. It was in her hands. If people relax and learn to flow with life, it always works out for the best. We learned that from our Appalachian Trail experience. Many wonderful coincidences happened to us in those six months. One hour after I had those thoughts, we found the two long-neck bottles of beer sitting dead center in the trail. An hour after that it began to rain driving us to find a motel. I guess Judy thought we were thirsty and needed to relax. You know, she was right.

We don't realize how much we rely on cars. Without one we are viewed as outcasts. Motel owners and restaurant personnel look at us distrustfully. They see us as vagrants with no means of support. We're viewed as being different which means people are cautious. People have built up so many barriers. I'm not saying this is all bad, but we have carried it to excess. When we enter an establishment, people are so quick to judge that they don't realize we are probably the most expensively dressed people there. For example, my backpack cost $475, raincoat $175, polypropylene shirt and pants $50, and boots $200. Not to mention sleeping bag and pad, stove, pots, gaiters, and hiking sticks. How many people do you know who wear a $1,000 outfit? Maybe we should leave the price tags on to make us more respectable.

While I'm on my soap box, I have noticed something else that becomes very apparent when I remove myself from everyday society for long periods of time. It seems from the time we're old enough to drive, we are bombarded with the message that it is OK or normal to be in debt. If you can't afford something, put it on your credit card. We receive at least two offers a week via mail or phone to take advantage of this great opportunity to have another credit card. Honestly now, why does anyone need more than one credit card? From mailing list to mailing list your name goes. It became apparent to me one time when my first name was misspelled. Somehow it got onto a list. Now I get card offers for Kitchard Freeman as well as for Richard Freeman. Another time I saved all the card offers sent to me for three months. Then added up the maximum loan I could receive from each. It came to over $500,000. I was tempted to max out those accounts and head to Belize, Central America.

Most people, when they have time on their hands, go shopping. They don't NEED anything, but it is fun to go to the mall as a hobby. When I take a look around our home, I see we also fell into the same hobby. Do we really need a TV and VCR in each room? We get caught up in the mind-set that bigger, faster, newer, and more will make our lives better. Of course we have to pay for all that stuff. So we work harder and longer hours. But then we don't have the time to enjoy all the stuff we worked so hard for. It is an ever upward vicious spiral. It wasn't until we did with so little while backpacking for six months, that we realized how much stuff we had. And most of it was more then we really needed. So we put a stop to it. We questioned everything we owned. Did we really need such an expensive house, cars, or lifestyle? It was nice to have them but at what price? We could still have a nice home at half the cost. Away with the new flashy sports car that we leased. Let the garage sale begin!

Sue's thoughts on a rainy day: I enjoyed the day of leisure, reading, writing, and watching TV. My feet began to heal and should be better tomorrow. I think Rich had too much time on his hands and shouldn't think so much!

Marauding Mosquitoes
August 22, Day 10

This morning we rose slowly, packed up for another day on the trail, and walked back up the road for a good breakfast at Clappison's Corners. We decided to skip a portion of road walk by going by taxi directly to Kilbride and picking up our mail drop. As we ate breakfast it began to rain again. Before picking up the phone to call a cab, Rich yelled out, "Anyone heading to Kilbride? My wife and I are hiking the Bruce Trail and need a ride." No immediate affirmative responses from the few locals, so we opened the phone book and located the number for the Waterdown Taxi. Then a voice from a table nearby rang out, "I'll give you a ride to Kilbride if you can wait a few minutes." We gratefully accepted. As it rained, we tossed our packs in the back of Jack's pickup truck and hopped in the cab. It turned out that Jack transplants trees around Ontario with a large spade truck, and his work today was stymied by the rain. We chatted all the way to Kilbride, which turned out to be a longer ride than we expected. Jack dropped us at the general store/post office, and we thanked him profusely.

The Kilbride General Store was a cute little place where the shopkeeper came out of the back-room bakery with

Sue sorts the mail drop on the porch of the
Kilbride General Store

flour on her hands to retrieve our package from the post office. We sorted our mail drop on the store's wide front porch, sheltered from the drizzle. We bought batteries and pita bread, filled two bottles with water, then set off laden with another heavy load. We expected a road walk but were pleasantly surprised to find the trail had been rerouted through a schoolyard and some fields.

As we eventually entered the woods, we became lunch for thousands of mosquitoes that swarmed around us, each trying to partake in the feast. Though we picked up the pace, swatted furiously, and wore bandannas as scarves, the mosquitoes were winning. Rounding a corner, we ran into an older couple also backpacking but heading south. Angels from heaven, they offered us some DEET, which we accepted and found instant relief! The four of us stood and chatted for quite a while, happy to see kindred souls. Originally from England, they now live in Manitoba and were doing about a quarter of the Bruce Trail. After exchanging experiences and the good things each of us should look forward to, we bid farewell and hiked on, much less bothered by the bugs.

DEET

> DEET, an abbreviation for N,N-diethyl-methatoluamide, is a bug repellent that works well on mosquitoes and less well on biting flies such as black flies, deer flies, or gnats. DEET is highly toxic and can dissolve plastics and synthetic fabrics. Care must be taken when using it.

Lunchtime break was at the Kelso ski chalet while we watched workmen clearing trees for a new ski run above us. Two trains came by just behind the chalet, which made Rich happy. He never tires of watching trains. We were sprinkled on a little this morning but nothing much. Ominous dark clouds kept blowing by, interspersed with patches of bright blue sky. The temperature was about 60°F (16°C), just right for hiking.

A pretty yellow finch perched on top of a thistle plant eating his fill of seeds as we marched through a field. We were amazed at how big and bushy the thistle plants grow here. At 5 p.m. we reached Halton Country Inn Golf Course. The backpacking couple we met this morning told us they had arrived here soaking wet and were offered a room for $10. So we thought … worth a try. Bob, the owner, wasn't in. His son was tending bar and told us that the rooms were normally long-term rentals, and he wasn't sure if his father had a vacancy or not. We ordered two Coors Light® beers and watched music videos at the bar for a while. The father hadn't returned by the time our glasses were empty so we headed out. Another option was to pay $5 to set up our tent on a nice manicured lawn back near the woods and trail. But after our relaxing drinks, we decided to continue on, adding a few more miles.

Just down the trail, Mother Nature reminded us who was boss by dousing us with a cloud dump, as we scrambled through a forest with cedar trees, some over 500 years old.

A forest of ancient cedars.

Ancient Cedars

In 1988, a professor from the University of Guelph discovered a 511-year-old Eastern White Cedar growing on a cliff face along the Bruce Trail. This was an astonishing find since cedars generally don't get much older than 100 years. It showed that the oldest forest in the eastern North America grows on the vertical cliff face of the Niagara Escarpment. The remains of a cedar over 1,500 years old were found on Flowerpot Island. It started life about the time King Tut was running Egypt.

The rock cliffs may not be the most hospitable place to grow but they are the safest. Growing in cracks and ledges, far from soil, and exposed to fierce winds, ice, falling rocks, and the baking summer sun, the cedars are small and twisted. But they don't have to withstand forest fires, logging, or aggressive neighbors trying to crowd them out or eat them.

Even along the top edge of the escarpment, the size of the cedars bears little resemblance to their age. A tree with a circumference of a few inches could be hundreds of years old. Clinging to the rock in harsh conditions, these stunted ancients have adapted well to their environment. Their tiny seeds can penetrate and grow even in the minute cracks in the rock.

We crossed a metal bridge spanning a large gap in the escarpment, which is now an active dolomite quarry. The dolomite is used to make cement and asphalt.

The trail today was fairly easy with many level walks. Tomorrow's looks to be much the same. My toes did well this morning but hurt again by lunch. Darn feet! We found a semi-level spot and pitched our tent, tired after a day of hauling heavy packs loaded from the recent mail drop. We lay in the tent reading, listening to the radio, and writing. All of a sudden the sky let loose and dumped rain. I bounded from the tent to gather all of our clothes, which were spread about to dry and air out. Buttoned up in the tent, we let the patter of rain lull us to sleep.

Through a Hole in the Wall

August 23, Day 11

A morning of plague and pestilence. We were awakened by sounds of large earth movers backing up .... beep, beep, beep. It was a chilly, windy morning. The rain had stopped, but the tent was still wet. We packed up, putting the tent in a plastic trash bag, and headed out wearing our fleece jackets and gaiters for warmth. The chill was fortunate for soon we entered the most lush stretch of poison ivy we had ever seen. There was no avoiding it, so it was a good thing we were wearing our gaiters. From there we entered a swampy stretch and became the hunted. Mosquitoes attacked from all angles. We dashed along, slapping and swatting. At 15th Sideroad, we decided to detour over to Speyside General Store to buy some bug repellent. DEET had become our ally.

Poison Ivy

Poison ivy is present in lush patches throughout the length of the Bruce Trail. Make sure you can identify it before hiking, because avoidance is the best means of defense. The leaves have a shiny, leathery texture and are always in clusters of three, prompting the old adage, "Leaves of three, let it be." Otherwise it's a diverse plant. The leaves can be green, red, yellow, orange, or even pink. Their edges can be saw-toothed or smooth. The leaves can be tiny or grow up to 4 inches (10 cm) long. Poison ivy grows as small plants, large clusters, or long vines. In places along the Bruce Trail, we saw plants knee high.

Poison ivy plants can be found deep in deciduous woods, along roadsides, and in open fields. All parts of the plant are toxic. Contact with the plant causes a nasty, blistered rash in 90% of the population. Even people who claim immunity will get the rash after multiple exposures to this weed. Only 2% of the population is truly immune.

The chemical component that people react to is an oily substance called urushiol. Twenty-four to 48 hours after contact a red, stinging rash will appear which develops into blisters. The urge to scratch is irresistible. Scratching itself doesn't spread the rash, because the blisters don't contain urushiol.

The best prevention is avoidance. But take our word for it, hiking along the Bruce Trail, you can't avoid poison ivy by trying to step around it. At times it almost covers the trail. You need some sort of protective clothing layer. We find hiking in pants too hot, so as soon as we spot the ivy, we don gaiters. Finally, remember not to touch the poison-ivy contaminated clothes until you can wash them in detergent. We gingerly fold the gaiters inside out until we can wash them.

Along the trail, jewelweed (touch-me-not) is also prevalent. Crush the entire plant and apply liberally to the skin immediately after exposure to poison ivy. The juice from the jewelweed neutralizes the urushiol and prevents a rash from forming. Or, if possible, scrub the skin with a strong soap as soon as possible.

Once blisters form, you can apply a variety of drugstore remedies, including calamine lotions, cortisone creams, and antihistamines which help minimize the itch. Extreme cases of poison ivy require a doctor's attention and usually cortisone shots.

The morning was dreary, cold, cloudy, wet, rocky, and buggy. The high point was an owl sighting. He spread his massive wings and flew silently through the forest. To me, it's one of the marvels of nature that a bird of that size can fly through a forest without making a sound. At another point, a grouse flushed from the brush right next to me and made me jump. This clumsy bird makes so much noise as it crashes into trees and brush trying to get away. What a contrast! The afternoon improved. The terrain remained flat, and we got out of the low wetlands. The sun even peeked out once in awhile. It's amazing how much affect

Down we go into the "Hole in the Wall."

the sun can have on our frame of mind.

We enjoyed the area called "Hole in the Wall" with its deep fissures between the rocks and a natural rock tunnel. I struggled today, having low energy, and limped into the Cedar Springs Motel on Highway 7 feeling like I'd done a 20-mile (32 km) day. In reality we'd covered only 13 miles (21 km) of little elevation change—nothing to brag about. Finding the motel room had a Jacuzzi® bathtub, I soaked in pure bliss thinking that this was how backpacking should be. But my small toes were still not cooperating. I had a large blister under each one. Rich was fortunate, not a single blister yet.

Snakes Alive
August 24, Day 12

We left the motel at 8 a.m. well rested and cleaner. It was cool, too cool for most of the mosquitoes. We had a peaceful walk through the rest of the lowlands. On both yesterday's trail and this morning's, the trail maintainers had constructed many board walks, maybe a half mile (0.8 km) in total length, making for a nice easy stroll. By 10 a.m. the sun was high in the sky and the thermometer said 60°F (16°C), but it felt warmer than that as we crossed through fields. This was my kind of morning. While Rich is a train person, I'm a cow person. As we hiked through several cow pastures and over many stiles, the cows glanced up at us then continued grazing, not minding our intrusion at all.

We could tell it was the weekend. Yesterday and today we'd seen many day hikers. They were generally quite friendly and stopped to talk to us. While we were sitting at the intersection of two dirt roads trying to determine our location, a young couple came by walking three dogs. When questioned, they had no idea where the Bruce Trail was. Seconds later an elderly lady came strolling by. She described exactly where we were, and where the Bruce Trail went. She had hiked this section of the trail often.

Later, as we sat on our packs, a rustle of leaves drew my attention to two finger-width snakes beside the trail. Yellow-and-black striped, they, like the cows, saw no need to scurry away from us, nor us from them.

Yellow-and-black Striped Snakes

Nine different types of snakes can be found along the Bruce Trail. Two very harmless yellow-and-black striped ones are the garter snake and the eastern ribbon snake. These two types are similar in appearance with lizard-like scales and large eyes, and can grow to lengths of 18 to 26 inches (46 to 66 cm). They eat small amphibians and fish and inhabit damp, swampy areas.

Both are harmless. If you pick one up, it may "poop" a foul-smelling gooey stuff on you. The garter snake can inflict a paper-cut-like bite. Ribbon snakes rarely bite.

Terra Cotta Conservation Area lived up to its name. A creek through it ran bright red from the terra-cotta clay bottom. We lunched in Terra Cotta at a picnic table while Canada geese played in the pond beside us. By 1 p.m. the mosquitoes woke up, and we donned our DEET armor in defense. The sun was now hidden behind a dense, dark, cloud cover. It looked like we were in for more rain. Weather conditions, like trail conditions, changed constantly, making for more interesting hiking.

Sure enough, as we hiked along, a steady sprinkle began. We suited up for rain, hiked for two more hours, then used our speediest method of tent erection. Basically that means keeping things as covered as possible and going like hell! Fortunately, the rain remained at a sprinkle, and we did pretty well at keeping things dry. It rained until 10 p.m., so instead of cooking in the rain, we each had a bowl of cold cereal for supper.

Listen to the
rhythm of nature
to find true peace.

Toxic Shirt
August 25, Day 13

Awoke to a faint glimmer of daylight and was surprised to read on my watch that it was 6:30 a.m. We had spent 14 hours in the tent. A peek outside revealed a world shrouded in fog. We reversed roles this morning. I was anxious to get up and about, Rich was groggy and would have preferred to go back to sleep. As three slugs crawled up the outside of our tent fly, Rich proclaimed himself "slug traffic coordinator" to ensure there were no mid-tent collisions.

All morning we marched along the wide, open-to-the-sky Caledon Trailway, thankful for the cloud cover. The trailway is flat, easy walking but would be unbearably hot on a sunny day. We raised our DEET shields against the mosquitoes once again. Rich saw a cormorant in a trailside swamp, and kingfishers squawked as we passed. To break the boredom, we sang Christmas carols but quickly quieted down as a day hiker got within earshot. By 11 a.m. we reached Caledon East. The trail passed right by the Lil' Miss Muffins Bakery and the pull was just too great. We stopped for sandwiches and juice and spread our tent and socks in the sun to dry. The sun was out for a few minutes then disappeared again, playing a game of hide and seek. We asked if there was a laundromat in town, but no such luck. I had washed most of our stuff in sinks a few times

Rich walks through a field of flowers along
the Caledon Trailway.

An easy stretch of trail along the Caledon Trailway.

along the way, but it's hard to get things dry unless we can lay them in bright sun for 15 to 30 minutes. Rich's shirt had turned "toxic." He went to hug me this morning, and the smell almost knocked me out. How could he stand himself? In desperation, he washed the shirt in the men's room sink and pinned it to the back of his pack to dry.

Cormorants

A large (25 to 36 inches long) black or very dark brown bird with a long, slender, hook-tipped bill. Cormorants dive for fish while on the water but not while in flight. They seldom remain under water more than 40 seconds. They're not as comfortable with water as many other birds and come ashore periodically to dry their feathers. Cormorants nest in colonies on cliffs and rocky islands.

Each step we took along the grass-lined path scared up 20 or so grasshoppers, providing a flurry of activity as we hiked along. Many had wings allowing them to fly 10 feet (3 m) at a hop. Another yellow-and-black striped snake crossed our path. Along a swamp, turtles sunned themselves on logs, and a great blue heron fished in the shallows. Then a treat. We walked right through a sheep farm. The sheep were beginning to grow wool coats after their summer shearing. Unlike the cows, the sheep weren't too happy at our intrusion and scurried away from us. We had to be sure to latch the gate at both ends of the farm to keep all of the animals in.

Palgrave was not a good choice for our mail drop. We had to follow Caledon Trailway past the Bruce Trail turn off, hike through a housing development, and climb a hill to find the post office. No other stores were near it or on the way. We would have done better using Caledon East as our mail-drop town.

We camped near the Palgrave Conservation Area in a lovely little woods with birch, cedar, pine, and maple trees as well as black-eyed susans. While we were at the post office, big black clouds blew in, and we thought we were in for another storm. But, the sky cleared. The weather sure changed fast around here.

Boo! Horses
August 26, Day 14

Neither of us was anxious to jump out of bed. The morning was a cool 55°F (13°C) and cloudy, and everything was wet with dew. But after we got hiking, it was a very pleasant walk through rolling hills. We've seen a series of reforestations (after logging). Some were 10 years old, some appeared to be 30 years old, and some mature pine forests. The forests were interspersed with fields full of late summer flowers and raspberries. Of course there were fewer berries after we passed through. Our boots were getting wet from the dew-laden grasses and weeds. We took our early morning candy bar break sitting on a bed of needles in a mature pine forest, smelling the fresh pine aroma, and listening to the birds chirping. We found that eating a Snickers® candy bar one hour into our hike gave us energy to hike until lunch.

The sun remained shielded behind clouds for the morning, keeping us cool. Still, we pulled into Mono Mills group campsite for lunch at the picnic table, drenched in sweat. The hills gave us an aerobic workout as well as views of a beautiful countryside dotted with groves of pine. We were serenaded during lunch by the crowing of roosters and cackling of chickens. While we ate, the clouds blew away, revealing a blue sky and hot sun.

On our hiking travels we have found that animals don't quite know what to make of backpacks. Friendly dogs have growled at us, and this morning we spooked two horses. Even though we moved well off the trail and stood very still as the horses and their riders passed us, the horses still reared and didn't want to go by.

Rich was getting trail weary and needed some pampering. He read that the Headwaters Hideaway Bed and Breakfast was nearby. After a short discussion we decided … why not? So we hiked on and headed into Mono Mills. It was a small crossroads town with a donut/deli shop, a grocery store, and a fish-and-chips restaurant. We ducked into the donut shop and called the B&B. They did have an opening, and the proprietor, Ed Burns, agreed to pick us up. Before long we were enjoying a refreshing shower and washing our smelly clothes. We spent the afternoon reading, relaxing, and generally being lazy.

In the B&B's backyard we cooked ourselves a hardy dinner of applesauce, green beans, spaghetti, and hot chocolate. Ed's wife, Lesley, was very friendly and saw to it that all our needs were met. After watching a little TV, we retired early and got a good long night's sleep.

All These Famous Glens
August 27, Day 15

With bellies full of eggs, bacon, toast, fresh fruit, juice, and coffee, we headed on our way north on 5th Line PHS to get back on the Bruce Trail. Although the Bruce Trail had many road walks in this section, we generally enjoyed them. They tended to be infrequently traveled dirt roads with quaint farms and houses. The countryside here was quite hilly, and the ridges that ran east/west reminded us of the blue ridges of Virginia.

A cloud cover again shielded us from direct sun, but the humidity was high, and we sweated profusely as we climbed the ridges and descended into deep ravines. We traveled fast through the wooded areas trying to outrun the mosquitoes. Neither of us wanted to use DEET after being freshly showered and laundered. Along the way, we did stop periodically to graze on the ripe raspberries and black-berries. I have a sharp eye for them and take every opportunity to collect a handful, never tiring of their taste. Rich tried a wild apple and said they were beginning to ripen and be palatable. The tops of each hill beckoned us with the sound of whistling leaves blown by a breeze. We would stand for a minute, arms outstretched enjoying the coolness.

The hills made this another beautiful area along the trail. We hiked around the perimeter of the Hockley Valley Golf Course. It looked like a fun one to play—all nestled in green mounds of earth. The golfers tooled around in carts on narrow pathways among the dramatic little hills. It would be a challenging course just to walk.

Crossing a stile, we entered a cow pasture. As we climbed and rounded each knoll, I kept asking Rich, where the cows were. Finally he said, "Short grass, cow plops, and cow smell, isn't that close enough?" "No," I replied, "that's like sitting and watching railroad tracks with no trains passing by." We achieved a perfect understanding using terms we each understood.

We had endured the morning's mosquitoes without using DEET, but we had both worked up a good sweat. By noon we crossed the Nottawasaga River, which was more the size of a good creek but clear, cool, and fast flowing all the same. We sponged off with bandannas to wipe away the sweat and cool our overheated bodies. It felt glorious! In the shade of a cedar tree along the river bank, we ate a lunch of rehydrated black beans in pita bread, ginger snaps, and dried fruit all washed down with Tang® orange-flavored drink.

The last few days had taken us away from larger cities and into the country. Gone were many of the sounds from cars, trains, and planes. All we heard now was the rustling of leaves as we walked through the deep woods or watched the swaying of grasses as we hiked up another beautiful hill. In many woods were small groupings of a plant commonly called doll's eyes. It is said the pioneers would dry the berries and use them for eyes in their homemade dolls. Every once in awhile we passed a lone red maple leaf lying on the path reminding us of the country were in and that fall would soon begin. Luscious mounds of lady ferns and maidenhair ferns abound in this enchanted forest.

White baneberry, commonly called dolls eyes.

Doll's Eyes

> White baneberry is a member of the buttercup family. It flowers in May and June with clusters of small white flowers. By fall it sports shiny white berries each with a black dot on thick red stacks. It's these berries, resembling the china eyes once used by pioneers for dolls, that caught our attention. The berries are very poisonous.

We've passed side trails with names such as Glen Haffey and Glen Cross. I thought, gee, Glen must be a very common man's first name in Canada. All these Glens have side trails named after them. Then it occurred to me. The Canadians use the term in reverse of what I'm used to. They mean glen as in ravine. In the U.S., we would say Haffey Glen or Cross Glen. Canada is not filled with honorable men named Glen after all.

We enjoyed Hockley Valley Provincial Nature Reserve. It began with a steep climb to a spectacular view of Hockley Valley. It's always fun to look back and see where we've been. Then the reserve went deep into woods with sharp ravines (or glens!) and cool, clear, running streams. It was a fun but exhausting walk. We took many breaks today to cool down. We decided we're not very good in high heat, and we're not very good in the cold. There's a narrow temperature range in which we operate optimally. But we decided, as we high-fived each other, We're good! We do get a bit cocky at times.

We did great today. Hiked strong until 6 p.m. and put in our longest mileage day yet—over 20 miles (32 Km)! As we prepared to brush our teeth after finishing dinner, an animal came strolling through the woods directly toward us. My first impulse was that it was probably a skunk, and we should take refuge in the tent. But Rich stood his ground, too curious to retreat. As the animal got closer we concluded that it was a porcupine. The feisty little fellow passed by within 25 feet (8m) of where we sat in front of our tent. Our intrusion didn't bother it one little bit.

Pass the Pasta, Please

August 28, Day 16

A quiet night. The porcupine did not return. I was concerned that it might circle back and gnaw on our boots, which were stashed in our tent vestibule. They're known for doing that, as they like the salt from human sweat.

Porcupine

Porcupines are nocturnal mammals with black or brown guard hairs on the front half of their bodies and backward pointing quills on the rump and tail. The 30,000 quills are modified hairs, which are solid at the tip and base, but with hollow shafts. They are loosely attached to muscles under the porcupine's skin. Porcupines don't actually throw their quills when attacked, they swing their tail to position the quills toward the enemy. Not known as fighters, porcupines would much rather retreat or climb a tree. When threatened, they will chatter their teeth as a warning sign before presenting their quills.

Porcupines walk with an unhurried waddle.

They are good, but slow, climbers using the
long claws on their forepaws. But, they have
been known to fall from trees. A full grown
porcupine can reach 40 pounds. They live in
deciduous, coniferous, and mixed forests and
are active all year round. If the winter gets
particularly cold, they may hole up in a rocky
bluff.

Porcupines eat twigs, green plants, and gnaw
on the bark of trees. They also gnaw on
human articles, such as boots, due to their
fondness for salt.

A fairly uneventful morning too. We walked through
woods, fields, and on dirt roads. The field walks were totally unmaintained except for the blazes telling us where to go.
At times we fought our way through chest-high vegetation,
often berry bushes and thistles full of prickers. I did graze
well on raspberries. We lunched near Highway 89. I picked
an open spot in an attempt to dry my soaked boots and
socks. The wet fields really drenched them, exacerbating
my problems. But the sky was overcast with only brief
pockets of blue sky and chances that my boots would dry
weren't good.

The trail in the Boyne River area was badly eroded. The
river itself was again a small creek, and we crossed easily
by rock hopping. Our climb out of the valley was reward-
ed with juicy ripe raspberries. Rich complained, "We'll
never get out of here!" I replied, "Just let me die in raspberry heaven." Then the work began—down and up

through four deep ravines. Pretty, but mighty difficult.

After crossing 1st Line EHS and another ravine, we came out to a farmer's fields then crossed through a wildflower field full of goldenrod, Queen Anne's lace, thistle, and even big pink cone flowers. The mood and view struck me, and I began dancing in circles singing the theme song from the movie *The Sound Of Music*.

Hiking on, we came upon a small, open-door cabin beside the trail. A sign on it said "Mulmur Hut" but no other indication of who owned it or who was allowed to use it. There was no mention of it in the maps, trail guide, or in the through-hiker's guide. It had a fire ring with benches around it, a picnic table, and even an outhouse. We had seen a spring just a few yards back. We had planned to go a bit further today, but with wet socks, my feet were really bothering me, so we decided to make this home for the night even though it was only 3 p.m. Hornets had already staked claim to the hut and it was pretty dirty, so we decided to set up our tent inside. That way we'd stay dry from either rain or dew, and the bees could have their space and we'd have ours.

Finally the sun came out and dried all of our clothes and boots. Tomorrow dry feet! I drained the blister on my big toe and bandaged it so it now felt better. Someone left two sections of a three-month-old *Toronto Star*, so we even got to read a newspaper. It was a nice, lazy afternoon.

Our appetites began to kick in. Dinners that were more than enough at the trip's beginning, now felt just like an appetizer. With five more days until our next mail drop in

Ravenna, we'd have to ration food. We scoured the maps and data, but didn't see any restaurants that we could visit. We'd definitely need to keep more of our food from the Ravenna mail drop.

Tonight we dined on hot strawberry Jell-O® gelatin and sour-cream-with-chives sauce on noodles—a Lipton dinner which is a backpacker's staple. It's a heck of a lot cheaper than freeze-dried meals. Lightweight and inexpensive, all of the Lipton dinners (pasta, noodles, rice) are quick and easy to fix on the trail and don't taste half bad.

A long-distance hiker's eating habits—primarily carbohydrate and sugar—are not a good diet for an average person. Foods we would never consider eating at home are a staple on the trail. Not only would our weight balloon, but our teeth would rot away. With our appetites increasing and sharing one pot, the unspoken game begins. How can I look like I'm eating my fair share, but really getting more? When Rich is cooking he needs to "test" the meal to see if it is ready. Then there's the "it's-too-hot-to-eat" ploy. Finally, he tries to divert my attention by saying something like, "Is that poison ivy behind you?" All just to get an extra spoonful. Maybe it's all part of the natural selection process.

Web Master
August 29, Day 17

Not a particularly restful night. We shared our home with a porcupine, at least we think it was a porcupine. We'd wake up to the sound of gnawing and shine our flashlight on the foodbag (suspended from the rafters under an upside-down tunafish can) to make sure something wasn't stealing our precious food. Mostly we figured the porky was under the hut. At one point, he or someone else walked across the roof.

We awoke in the morning to heavily overcast skies and dew-covered fields. Drat! I figured my dry feet would be wet within half hour. But, it wasn't all that bad after all. However, we discovered as we packed up that my gaiters were missing. We haven't a clue as to how or when we lost them. We try to be careful and survey the ground behind us after we camp or stop for a break. Maybe they fell off a pack while we hiked. If it rains or gets cold now, I'm in trouble.

We got an early-morning workout up and down, up and down, up and down. After crossing many more streams than were on the map, we had no idea where we were until we reached 8 Sideroad. A long road walk was cut short as the rerouted trail veered off into the woods. Reroutes off roads are important to improve the trails. All of a sudden we were back into escarpment rocks and cliffs. We'd been hiking on regular woods, fields, and dirt paths for quite some time now. But the escarpment had returned. We got our first glimpse of a cave and crossed over a natural rock bridge.

The walk down Center Road into Kilgorie was our favorite road to walk so far—tree-shaded, narrow gravel road which wound downhill gradually. Beside it, one side stream after another joined the main stream on its tumble and gurgle down a sandy-bottom creek bed. On our way down, it started to sprinkle, so we donned pack covers, only to have the sun come back out. I sure hoped there would be a restaurant in Kilgorie. We needed a reward for all of the elevation loss which would have to be regained.

Nature had been playing with us this past week. In the mornings it was heavy overcast. Then, as the days wore on, it began to clear. Rich would speak enthusiastically about the blue skies. Then just as quickly, black clouds would come across the horizon, and Rich would change his prediction. Then just as quickly, the clouds would pass, giving us new hope again. And so each day went. Normally, we would hardly notice the weather, but in the woods, each change is dramatic.

A tough afternoon. The Mulmur area was very hilly, so we spent the afternoon either sliding steeply down, climbing steeply up, or thrashing through chest-high berry bushes complete with prickers.

I was having trouble seeing through cobwebs embedded

on my glasses. Each morning we denoted the lead walker for the day, or the "web master." Every couple of minutes that person walked through cobwebs requiring her or him to wipe sticky webs from face and arms. Actually, the extra arm waving helped me stay awake. From a distance though, I'm sure it looked quite strange. Sometimes I walked first, but because I'm shorter, I missed some webs. Consequently, Rich felt he might as well go first and save me from this minor irritation. Who says chivalry is dead?

By 3:30 p.m. we stumbled hot, sore, and tired to the Mulmur House Bed and Breakfast. Proprietors John and Carol Cholvat welcomed us. We felt so much better (and smelled better too) after a shower.   All of our clothes went in the washer, their second official laundering since we left home 17 days ago. The main part of Mulmur House was built in 1905. The restoration and addition received the Niagara Escarpment Achievement Award and reflected a relaxing, early-Canadian style. After seeing the before

The delightful Mulmur House Bed and Breakfast.

pictures, we knew why they received the award.

Carol and John invited us to join them for dinner. Or, we could cook one of our trail meals out on their patio. Since our appetites had grown, and we could use our trail food to double up a meal, we said yes to the real home-cooked meal. Over chicken, baked tomato, rice, salad, apple pastry with real maple syrup, and coffee, we enjoyed delightful conversation.

Which Way, Kemosabe?

August 30, Day 18

*T*he morning breakfast would bring a smile to any hiker's face. We feasted on cheese omelets, bacon, fresh fruit, fresh-baked croissants and jam, fresh-baked banana-blueberry muffins, orange juice, and coffee, all done with gourmet presentation.

The Mulmur House was a hard place to leave. When we finally did move on, we were instantly sorry. The first stretch heading north had us again thrashing through waist-high brush and prickers. The morning dew drenched us. Then we came to a farm lane and had difficulty telling which way the trail went. We walked for awhile then back-tracked. After checking the maps, we decided to head down the farm lane again. It was a long way before we finally saw a blaze that confirmed our route. Then reaching a fork, we saw no blazes. Rich went one way and I went the other. Eventually I found a blaze facing south, none facing north, and yelled to Rich that I had the trail. What we were on, we would come to know as the dotted line section of the 1st Line EHS. It was a delightful, narrow dirt roadbed, shaded by trees, but it was exasperating to walk because the blazes were so few and far between. Even when we reached the corner at Baseline Road, there was no indication of which way to turn and no blazes in sight. Too many times we've walked the obvious path only to learn that the trail had veered into the woods somewhere, and we had missed the turn requiring us to backtrack. So we were constantly on our guard.

Dave Shepherd, one of the many trail maintainers.

We stopped for our morning candy bar break on the grass in front of the quaint Lavender Cemetery, established in 1880. As we reentered the woods just past the hamlet of Lavender, we met Dave Shepherd with axe in hand. He explained that this wasn't his section, but he was working on it because it was overgrown. His section was further in a bit, and he assured us that we would find it in good shape. We thanked him for his work in maintaining the trail. True to his word, the trail ahead was well trimmed and expertly blazed.

The trail now took us along the edge of the escarpment through cedar forest. Huge chunks of moss covered rock had pulled away from the main ledge. The view over the edge was of a rolling valley with lush farm fields of various colors. We could tell it was the weekend because we again met groups of people doing the Bruce Trail in sections. We were beginning to see more and more fall colors peek through with yellows, rusts, and reds. Rich continued to test the wild apples with each tree we passed. Most were still bitter, but he found one tree this morning that he claimed was good eating.

We lunched at the ponds just south of Eden shelter. The sun came out from behind the clouds, so our walks down Dunedin Road and up Concession 10 were hot. We wore our sun hats and wished for the breeze from previous days.

Farmers were busy in their fields harvesting the golden wheat. At one point we came over a stile as a farmer was turning a corner in his field comfortably enclosed in the air-conditioned compartment of his combine. We crossed below his field through deep grasses and thistle on an incline. Traversing the hill was difficult in the deep weeds. We could see raised blazes ahead so we knew where to go, but getting there was no easy task. Periodically we found a trampled area, but most of the time there was no discernible path. The footing was uneven and it had me spooked. I really don't like walking when I can't see where I'm placing my feet.

I was glad to leave that field and progress to another where the weeds were lower. A groundhog greeted us. Standing on his hind legs surveying his turf, he remained upright until we were within six feet (2 m) of his hole, then he dove quickly for cover. We set our sights on a creek as a water source for the night, hoping to fill up and quickly find a

place to camp. But the creek didn't exist, and we found ourselves on a road past where the water should have been, hot
and tired. No choice but to push on. Fortunately the next
stream on the map did have water. We filled up and had a
quick bandanna bath.

We nestled in a cedar forest, not very far off the trail. Next
to us was a very old hand-hewn split-rail fence, which uses
angled wooden braces for support rather than posts or nails.
We slept on a soft bed of cedar needles with the aroma of
cedar overpowering our usual sweaty smell. We ran
through an "invisible" procedure. Our preference was that
no one sees, hears, or knows where we're camping, for safety reasons. Rich calls it stealth camping. While our stove
was boiling water for dinner, we heard voices down the
trail. Rich turned off the stove, and we both sat quietly
while a young couple marched by. We could easily see
them, and if they had looked, they could have seen us,
especially since our brightly colored bandannas and packs
and the rest of our hiking clothes were hanging on cedar tree
branches to air out. But these hikers, as most, were con-
centrating on the path before them and talking about flowers along the trail. They never noticed our presence. As
their voices dimmed in the distance, we resumed our dinner
preparations. Rich stowed all our colorful stuff because the
couple was probably out for a Saturday evening stroll and
would have to return this way.

We have found that not only is stealth camping fun but so
is stealth hiking. The woods and fields are perfect with
their own sounds. Any noises that we make are only dis-
cordance. Hiking quietly allows our thoughts to wander or

our ears to hear the natural sounds. Plus we have a much better chance of seeing animals if we walk quietly. It's harder than it seems. Since this was my first trek using hiking sticks, I tended to click and clang them on rocks and roots. Rich would glare back at me periodically with a look that said, "Quiet down!"

In the last few days we began seeing flocks of Canada geese. They bedded down at night in the wheat fields and flew just over our heads heading south for the winter. They looked like they were having fun honking back and forth, gliding so effortlessly over the escarpment. Wouldn't it be wonderful to have wings to fly down into the lush green valley below dotted with red barns and green roofs?

Bruce Trail
(Northern Half)

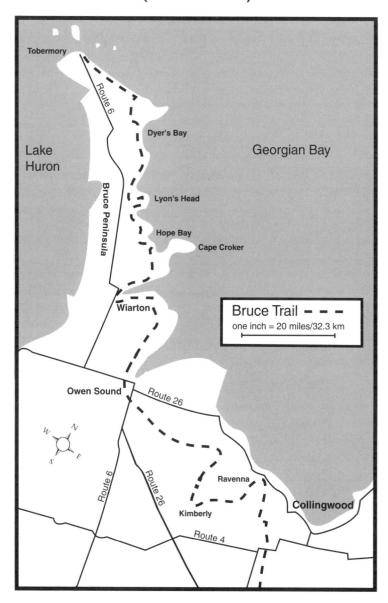

Tobermory

Route 6

Lake
Huron

Bruce Peninsula

Dyer's Bay

Georgian Bay

Lyon's Head

Hope Bay

Cape Croker

Wiarton

Bruce Trail ▬ ▬ ▬
one inch = 20 miles/32.3 km

Owen Sound

Route 26

N
W   E
S

Route 6

Route 26

Ravenna

Kimberly

Collingwood

Route 4

Company for Dinner
August 31, Day 19

We spent last night close by a pack of coyotes. We had settled in just after dusk, and the woods were silent. Then suddenly a chorus of howls began, lasting about a minute. Then, eerie silence. A farmer must have heard them also and released two of his dogs to watch over his land. They came barking into a pasture in the valley. Four times the coyotes howled, the last time at dawn.

Coyote

Coyotes have adapted well to life in southern Ontario and are located all along the Bruce Trail. But, it's rare to see one. They are sly animals and avoid human contact as much as possible. The best possible sighting times are fall and winter evenings and early mornings when both young and adult coyotes are busy traveling in search of food.

You're much more likely to hear their high-pitched howls punctuated with short barks and a multitude of yips, the kind of sound that sends a chill down your spine. But, enjoy nature's music; coyotes are not a threat to humans. They howl to communicate during hunting, to greet pack members, or to seek a lifelong mate. Try a few howls before settling to sleep at night. If coyotes are in the area, they commonly will answer your howl right away.

Coyotes are dog-like animals with a tawny-gray fur and a black-tipped tail. They weigh 50 to 60 lbs. (23 to 27 kg) and eat small prey such as rabbits and rodents. If necessary, they've been known to eat deer, fruit, berries, vegetation, garbage, and domestic animals such as sheep, cattle, and cats. Their primary social unit is a mating male, female, and their pups under a year old.

Before the Europeans came to America, the coyote was a plains animal, inhabiting southwestern North America. They migrated to Ontario in the early 1900s and were considered plentiful by the 1940s. They adapted well to the increase in agricultural lands and human encroachment.

We awoke early this morning to the patter of rain. Rich reached out, zipped down our fly, and nestled back to sleep. He rustled again and asked me to check the time. It was 6:45 a.m. even though little sun filtered through the tent. It sprinkled lightly on us as we packed up and as we hiked the morning hours. We climbed up the escarpment and again had views of the fertile farms in the valley below. We passed a group of two cars, four tents, and young men just in the throes of getting up for the day. They had camped along the edge of the escarpment in an area that contained caves. Later we checked the map—there were no roads shown to that area. The men must have known some farm lane that wasn't mapped.

As we wandered down an old dirt lane, a mole scurried across the road in front of us. Then came a larger animal, about the size of a porcupine but with a much deeper brown coat. We didn't get a good look at his tail, but maybe it was a beaver. As we reached the base of Devil's Glen Ski Resort, the sky opened up with a good downpour. We ducked under the eaves of a building hopefully to wait out the storm. We couldn't go inside; it was closed for the summer.

I was apprehensive now. We were heading into snake country. People kept warning us that this year the Eastern Massassauga rattlesnakes had bitten more people than usual. That's another reason I particularly like being able to see where I step.

The challenge: A new, very wet drainage ditch to cross.

After about 15 minutes, the rain stopped and we headed onward across the Mad River and up the side of the glen. We faced our first real obstacle in a field past Highway 24. The farmer, with a backhoe, had dug a drainage ditch 10-foot (3 m) wide around his property. With the rain, the ditch was full of water and very wet clay. Rich tested it with his hiking stick, and the stick sunk three feet down. We walked along the edge of the ditch collecting flat boulders to toss into the water. We had to pile several on top of each other to make stepping stones that would be stable enough for us to cross. Our hiking sticks were useless for balance because they just sunk in the mire beside us. We both managed to get across without falling into the mud, although I'll never win any awards for gracefulness.

Hiking Sticks

In recent years, hiking sticks have become popular in the U.S. Non-hikers still give us strange looks. "Where are your skis?" ceases to be funny after a while. But it remains the predominate question asked as we encounter day hikers and people in towns. Actually, I use old ski poles (cut to a shorter length and minus the snow baskets). Rich uses expensive hiking sticks complete with spring compression and tungsten-carbide tips.

We've found that hiking sticks improve our balance when we clamor over obstacles and help us maintain a walking rhythm. We can also use them to hold back wet bushes, barbed wire, stinging plants, and other trail obstructions.

Dr. Gottfried Neureuther of Munich did research on the use of hiking sticks. He measured the load weight on the sticks during flatland walking and found that the load was relieved on the lower extremities and spine about 45 times per minute or 7,000 times per hour at an average of 5 kg (11 lbs) and even more if walking uphill or downhill. His research found that an enormous burden is taken off the lower body per hour of hiking: 13 tons on flatland, 28 tons uphill, and 34 tons downhill.

Some people use just one stick, but the research of Professor Reich Muller of Salzburg showed that using two sticks reduced the load on joints. From personal experience, we can tell you that the use of two sticks significantly reduces the stress on knees. So let them laugh at us. We'll be like the Energizer Bunny® and just keep going and going and going with hiking sticks in hand.

The road walks along Concession 10 and Duntroon Road were long. Many cars zipped by us. The saving grace was that half way down Concession 10, we found a home bakery. We knocked on the door, and a very pleasant young woman waited on us while her toddler scurried around behind her. The four butter tarts we purchased were consumed with relish before we reached Duntroon Road, and they gave us the energy needed to climb the escarpment and hold out until lunch. The afternoon walk was much more pleasant through Nottawassga Lookout and down a road allowance. After the Singhampton Side Trail, we began heading toward the highest point on the trail. Rich wanted to know why the highest point on any trail is always preceded by a long steep down. I had no answer as we continued downhill.

We could never tell what dotted-line roads on the map (often called road allowances) would be like. Sometimes they were untouched forest. Others have been summer-only gravel roads, farm lanes, field paths, and even wooded paths. The roads laid out in square grids were also new to us. At home the pioneers built the roads along the path of least resistance, so they wander all over. Here roads were straight as arrows. If a large hill (like the escarpment) was in the way, the roads went straight over it, no messing around. They seemed to be laid out with true military precision.

Split-rail fences were ever present. They were beside us as we walked the fields and beside us as we wandered in the woods—mile after mile, designating past and present boundaries. They represent history for this land. Each time we walked beside them we wished they would tell their story. Why, when, and by whom were they built? How much sweat equity went into their existence? You could learn so much from them about the families that gave their souls to this land. Most fences were four or five rails high, but a few were seven rails high. We wondered what kind of animals were being raised that warranted the extra work to build such a high fence?

We chose a campsite and set up as usual. Rich began

A country road, straight as an arrow
even when the escarpment was in the way.

Split-rail fences were very common along
the central section of the Bruce Trail

preparing dinner and I was sorting food, when Rich said, "We have company," and pointed up in a nearby tree. Sure enough, an animal was huddled in the branches toward the top of the young spindly tree about 15 feet (4.6 m) ahead of us and 15 feet in the air. We had a stare down but couldn't quite figure out what it was. No stripes of a raccoon or skunk. No quills of a porcupine. We considered an opossum, but our friend's monkey-like face was brown and flat, not pink and pointed. It had a beautiful brown fur coat. Rich halted dinner preparations joking that he just couldn't create a gourmet meal with an animal's eyes watching his every move. Mind you he was cooking a Lipton Noodle-Stroganoff® dinner. Not exactly haute cuisine. However, he resumed cooking, and we continued to watch our visitor. It moved very slowly, sometimes stretching a paw, scratching its belly once, moving to another branch. It had a furry, fluffy brown tail about six-inch (15 cm) long. We still didn't know what it was, but it was the best dinner entertainment we'd had yet.

Our backpacks and tent were getting dirtier as the trip wore on. Damp, rainy days hastened the process. The tent was not only dirty, but bloody. Each night a few more mosquitoes that slipped into the tent were squished against the netting, adding a colorful spot.

Ice Cream at Last

September 1, Day 20

We slept until 7:30 a.m. and lay in our sleeping bags lazily listening to the birds and squirrels playing outside the tent. Our dinner visitor was gone when we got up; it snuck away under the veil of darkness. We still didn't know what it was and would have to research it at the library. On the trail by 8:30 a.m., we climbed out of the Pretty River valley. At the first pinnacle, the view was of valleys shrouded in low clouds. The trail took us down again and then criss-crossed tributaries to the Pretty River—a very picturesque walk along streams that babbled over rocks and cascaded over fallen trees. Another long climb brought us to our break spot at the highest point on the Bruce Trail. Now even we were shrouded in dense clouds.

Since it was Labor Day, I was sure we'd see people. We had already seen three. They flew effortlessly down on mountain bikes, while we puffed and sweat on our climb up. Thrashing through wet leaves, we joked that we got our morning shower. It was like driving through a human car wash.

After the trail's highest point, our reward came in a long, level section. I was glad the next day was resupply day. I needed to load Rich down with heavy food again. With a light pack he moves too fast. We scrambled through mossy escarpment boulders south of 2nd Line and then climbed through them straight up the face of the escarpment north of 2nd Line. The sun had now burned off the morning fog, and the temperature was up from the high 50s to almost 70°F (21°C).

North of 2nd Line the trail was rerouted, so it didn't follow the map. It was a nice route except for three things. The last part was a boggy mess with murky mud to wade through. It was blazed only southward so we had to keep searching behind us to make sure that we were still on the right trail. And, it emptied us onto busy Grey County Road 19. On the hot, sunny walk down Grey County Road 19, we got a glimpse of Nottawasaga Bay (off Georgian Bay) through the haze to the east. We could clearly see the escarpment ledge that we walked yesterday.

Turning off Grey County Road 19, we headed uphill and picked the third stream crossing for lunch. One side was an open field, the other side was woods. We could wash up, eat in the shade of the woods, and dry our socks in the sunny field; that was the theory. In reality, a big gray cloud blew in so there was no sun for my socks. Ten minutes after we were finished eating and on the trail again, the sun came out in full force. Life's not fair! After lunch the trail continued on tough terrain. A long climb up then a long climb down on a gravel road, then back up to the top of the escarpment again. On the Appalachian Trail we called these PUDs for "pointless ups and downs."

Heading down a dusty back road, we passed a group of 25 Mennonite people, mainly teenagers with a few adults and two smaller children. The boys were dressed in the traditional Mennonite long-sleeved blue shirts and black pants. The girls had long-sleeved dresses with black tights and bonnets. A sharp contrast to Rich in only his shorts and me in shorts and jogbra. They asked us where the trail was, saying they were on a bus trip and were taking a hike for fun. We gave them directions, and Rich asked the adults if they had water. One of the boys had a canteen, but it was empty, so we filled it for them with our treated water.

Our last leg back up the escarpment was a road walk on Scenic Caves Road. A glance behind us gave a panoramic view of Collingwood in the valley and Georgian Bay complete with an island lighthouse. Then as we progressed IT appeared. The most welcome tourist area I've ever set eyes upon—Collingwood Scenic Caves. In unison Rich and I spotted a sign and sang out, "Ice cream!" We made a beeline for it and ordered not only chocolate ice cream cones, but cheeseburgers and orange juice as complements. It tasted so good. Both of us had growing appetites and a dwindling food supply.

After Scenic Caves, we followed the edge of the escarpment past the tops of two ski resorts. The views to the bay below were fantastic. One large building, a grain elevator, was particularly noticeable. Patches of bright fall colors signaled autumn's approach. At the end of the day, as I sat on the woods floor writing my log, the brown leaf base was sprinkled with red and yellow leaves of autumn.

Rich was in a grumpy mood today. By the end of the day, he said his feet hurt and he was going home. I said, "No way! I need you out here with me. I could never carry all the stuff needed to do a solo backpacking trip. Besides it would be too lonely to do by myself." *He'll be in a better mood tomorrow.*

Spending long periods of time with your spouse can be quite trying. Oh sure, you love him or her, but being within ten feet of that person, twenty-four hours a day is a test for any marriage. However, these conditions were different because each of us was carrying something essential that the other needed. For example, Rich had the food and tent, while I had the stove, pot, and fuel. So we were constantly reminded that this truly was a team effort, and that was the glue that bound us through the rough times.

A Surprise at Ravenna

September 2, Day 21

The weather forecast (per Rich's radio) said storms were coming. Overnight the wind picked up, and we expected it to rain before morning. A lone coyote howled as we settled in to sleep—nature's music. We awoke to a perfect hiking day at 6:15 a.m., packed in a hurry, and were on the trail by 7 a.m. It was 64°F (18°C) with a 20 mph (32 kph) breeze and a blue sky with cirrus clouds. Our intent was to get to Ravenna as early as possible. The through-hikers' guide said there was no public phone at the post office/general store, but we figured if we were drenched when we reached there, we might be able to convince the proprietors to let us use their private phone to call a bed-and-breakfast.

We hiked along and watched the sun rise over the escarpment. In a dry stream bed, we found a perfect example of a natural flowerpot. As we hiked, the blue sky clouded over and the wind continued to pick up. With our westward walk toward Ravenna, the wind was directly in our faces. Thank goodness, no rain yet.

A natural flowerpot along the trail.

Flowerpot

A flowerpot, or sea stack, is a vase-shaped pillar of stratified rock formed when Lake Nipissing, an ancestor to Lake Huron, covered the area about 5,500 years ago.   Lake Nipissing was formed from glacial meltwaters and was 56 feet (17 m) higher than the current lake levels.   As wave action pounded against the sides of rock shoreline that jutted into the lake, the softer limestones eroded away leaving a tall island of rock, the flowerpot.

Flowerpots generally have dolomite caps and softer limestone bases.   The rock was formed about 440 million years ago from the skeletons of marine animals who lived at the bottom of a shallow inland sea.

Devil's Monument (44 feet or 13 m tall) is the only documented Lake Nipissing-level flowerpot on the Bruce Peninsula.   Flowerpot Island, in Georgian Bay off the northern end of the Bruce Peninsula, has two flowerpots, one 50 feet (15 m) tall, and the other 30 feet (9 m) tall.   Smaller flowerpots are found elsewhere along the escarpment.

We stuck our thumbs out on the last stretch of road walk into Ravenna. Two trucks and a car passed us by. The third truck, containing a woman and small child, stopped. The woman said Ravenna was only two minutes away, just down the hill, but she'd give us a ride anyway if we still wanted one. We accepted and rode on the tailgate of the truck while it zipped down and down and down. We hopped out at the Ravenna four corners and thanked the woman. She had saved us at least a half hour of road walk even though to her it was only a two-minute jaunt.

The Ravenna General Store,
run by Larry and Rosemary Morton.

The Ravenna General Store turned out to be a delightful surprise and a very busy place. Larry and Rosemary Morton, who have owned it for less than two years, not only operate the post office, general store, gas pumps, and a bed-and-breakfast, but they make and sell scrumptious pies and have their home here. The original structure was built in 1870 and has had two additions. The general store portion just celebrated its 50th anniversary.

We picked up our mail drop and prepared a package to send home our exposed film, daily logs, and excess food. Larry and Rosemary were curious about the package we had mailed to ourselves. They provided cups of coffee to sip as we sorted our mail drop. Before heading on our way, we bought bread and two homemade butter tarts for the road. Larry volunteered to drive us back to the trail, and Rich joked, "How about driving us to Owen Sound? I'm anxious to get a shower and a good meal!" That's when Larry mentioned their bed-and-breakfast service. It's taken them awhile to get things up and running here, and they only began the bed-and-breakfast this spring. To me it was a no-brainer. We had looked at the options going forward, and there really wasn't anything conveniently close to the trail until Owen Sound, which would be five to six days off. Outside the air was getting thicker and chillier, and although it still wasn't raining, it felt as though it could start any minute. Our feet were already soaked from wet field walks this morning. Besides, we were in no hurry, why not enjoy this trek and take advantage of every opportunity as it was presented. We decided to stay.

By 11 a.m. we had each showered and hand-washed some clothes, and were sitting in upholstered chairs sipping coffee and eating our butter tarts with a whole day of rest ahead of us. Rich was definitely in a much better mood now.

The proprietors told us that this was their retirement. They purchased the establishment with visions of a simple, laid-back life, where they could talk with the local people and enjoy the common pleasures. Like all visions, this one was somewhat idealized. As we sat in their comfortable living room sipping coffee, a series of bells rang, each one designating a customer in need of service. Each customer was greeted by name. A car drove up to the gas pumps and ran over a black hose. Ding-ding went a bell, and Larry or Rosemary ran outside to pump gas. Ding-dong announced a customer entering the store for groceries or for the post office located in the rear corner. We heard a hardy "Hi," and the morning's load of mail arrived for sorting. Then the phone rang, and a customer asked if his priority package had arrived. Next there was baking to be done, products to be ordered, and shelves to be stocked. Ahhh retirement!

Rosemary cooked two meals for us. Ham sandwiches and pea soup for lunch and pot roast, potatoes, gravy, and lots of vegetables for dinner. It all tasted so good. We watched the movie *Jerry McGuire* on the VCR and snuggled together as wind drove rain against the windows; we were glad to be inside. Before we knew it, it was pitch black outside and well beyond our usual bedtime.

Ravenna was just a dot on the map and a small one at that! We had enjoyed our conversation with Larry and Rosemary, especially about their experience buying and running a small business. We were thankful to them for showing us a slice of their lives. How many times have we driven through these little places never thinking of the families who live there?

On the Road Again
September 3, Day 22

After a big breakfast, Larry drove us down the road to the trail crossing. By our 9:30 a.m. start, it had warmed up to 50°F (10°C) with a brisk, strong wind, and the sun streaming through puffy clouds. We started out wearing our fleece jackets, but soon the blood surged through our veins, and we shed the outer layer, once again hiking in shorts and polypropylene T-shirts. The walk began with the common alternation between pastures, fields, and forests, then took us into a playland. We descended the escarpment through a gap in the solid stone walls. We had to toss our hiking sticks ahead and use all hands and feet to lower ourselves through the crevices. Hemlock and birch trees clung to tiny ledges on the sheer white rock walls. This section from County Road 2 to 10th Line (just before Kolopore Creek) would make a nice short hike for anyone looking to experience a fun section of the Bruce Trail.

A gorgeous day for hiking, by noon the temperature reached 60°F (16°C) with a strong, north wind and not a cloud in the sky. A clear, crisp day, we could see across to the escarpment cliffs that we'd already climbed and also the bay to the north. Even major climbs didn't get us all sweaty today. We passed another home bakery on Sideroad 10D, but believe it or not, we didn't stop. We'd been fed so well at Ravenna, including home-baked raspberry pie a la mode, that our craving for food just wasn't the same as it had been.

The escarpment wasn't the solid wall of rock that I had envisioned. From Niagara through Hamilton, it was a big long ridge, and we walked below, above, or across the face of it. But in this central area, the escarpment was in chunks, often separated by eroded areas which were now farmlands. Sometimes, we didn't even realize that we were near the cliff edge. We'd hike along through a pasture or field, and then escarpment rocks or a drop off would suddenly appear on one side.

Our feet, particularly my feet, were doing well today. All my blisters were healed or healing, and I had dry socks and boots. Even the field walks today were well trodden, so I didn't get soaked from yesterday's rain or last night's dew. Rich mentioned this morning that his boots felt like well worn slippers. It only took 1,000+ miles (1,609 km) to get them that way. There's nothing like a properly fitting boot.

Our bodies, too, were getting worn in. No expensive gyms for us. We prefer to exercise outside in the beauty of nature. No 45-minute aerobics class in fashionable shorts and top, but a six to seven hour hike each day. After three weeks we began to feel in shape. If the trail went up a steep cliff, our only thought was to place our bodies in low gear and do it. It felt good to be able to maintain the rhythm for hours on end, controlling our breath and hardly missing a beat to take a swig of water or a handful of gorp. This was the feeling all long-distance hikers strive for.

It was a long, road walk afternoon. Hard on the bottoms

of our feet and not much to look at. At least we didn't bake in the sun. In the Old Baldy Conservation Area, we followed along the edge of a cliff with good views of Beaver Valley. I suspected it would be even prettier on the other side when we were looking back. People continued to be much friendlier up here. Maybe it's just the difference of rural vs. suburban. It reinforced my desire to live a more rural lifestyle.

Good thing it was cool now. It meant we needed less water, because we didn't sweat as much. We were running low on iodine tablets, and we had five or six days of hiking until our mail drop at Owen Sound. I've sent two bottles home already because we weren't using them, especially through the early sections when the creeks were dry, and we had to ask for water at houses. I thought I had put a bottle in each mail drop, but there wasn't one in the Ravenna drop. There had better be one in the Owen Sound drop. For the Appalachian Trail hike, I put a list in each mail drop telling me what would be in the next drop. That way I could plan ahead and know if I should keep something or send it home. I wish I had done that for this trip.

More road walk—much too much for any one day. The bottoms of our feet hurt, and for some reason, my knee was bothering me too. We misjudged a camping spot for the first time. We thought that we could camp in the flat area around Beaver River, but it turned out to be the entrance to Beaver Valley Ski Resort. So we stopped at the resort, filled up with water (so we didn't have to use any iodine tablets), and slogged up the ski runs. Then we had to go quite a distance because the trail ran next to ski chalets and on the side of the hill. This time I was the grumpy one because I was carrying three of the four quarts of water up from the ski resort, and I was already sore and tired.

But we did make better mileage today and found a good place to camp, so it turned out fine. Rich cooked us a dinner of fetuccine alfredo and hot passion-fruit Jell-O® gelatin. I looked forward to snuggling into the warmth of our tent. The thermometer said 50°F (10°C), and the wind was still strong.

Here, Little Mousy

September 4, Day 23

Burr, a cold night. We kept warm, though, in our sleeping bags with bandannas on our heads. It was tough getting out of bed in the morning. Luckily, the wind had died down and the sun was out. It was 42°F (5°C) when we stepped foot on the trail at 8:09 a.m. Once more it didn't take long before we warmed up and shed the fleece jackets.

Mystery solved. We now know that the beaver-like animal we saw cross the road and our treed dinner visitor were both porcupines. We got a close look at one clinging to a tall bush beside the trail this morning. They do have thick brown fur covering the quills, furry tails, and dark monkey-like faces. Shortly after meeting Mr. Porcupine, three deer ran across the trail in front of us. We sat at the top of the escarpment having our morning break, about to cross a stile and march through a field of grazing cattle. Only 9:30 a.m. and it had already been a great day for viewing wildlife.

We hiked back into the woods and descended the escarpment cliff on a ladder, then walked along the base of sheer rock cliffs for awhile. At our morning break, after we had climbed out of Beaver Valley then looped down and up again, Rich said the worst of the day was behind us. Going forward the map looked like docile land. But for two more hours we labored, through rough terrain before it settled into rolling farmland. Maybe it's just that I was a sloth today, but for some reason my energy level was low.

Rich said I played martyr yesterday by carrying three bottles of water when we filled up at Beaver Valley Ski Resort. What gets into the psyche that makes you think you have to carry more than your fair share? It happens to all of us. It was my turn. "I am woman, hear me roar!"

It continued to be a perfect hiking day, clear and cool. We had great views of the wide, sweeping Beaver Valley with its farms and ski runs. At lunchtime we picked the corner of a field with access to sun and shade and no extra charge for the panoramic view of the valley. In the afternoon it warmed up to almost 70°F (21°C). We peeled off our shirts and hiked in the cool breeze. Our valley views changed to bay views. The royal blue water glistened under baby blue skies, surrounded by the lush greens and yellows of forests and fields. Farmers were busy with the harvest again today.

We put dehydrated peas in a bottle with some water this morning to rehydrate. All day long I assumed Rich was carrying them. Then I found out, no, I was carrying them. No wonder I was a slug—I had a whole five ounces (142 grams) of extra weight. We ate the peas for our afternoon break, plump, juicy, and cold. Later, we filled three bottles with water from a spring. Normally we'd treat even spring water, but due to our shortage of iodine pills, we risked drinking it untreated.

Giardia

The stream or pond water may look crystal clear, but what you can't see, can hurt you. Lurking inside is probably a protozoa or one-celled bacteria called giardia lamblia (pronounced gee-are-dya lam-blee-a) or giardia for short.

Giardia causes a disease called giardiasis with symptoms including one or more of the following: diarrhea, fever, cramps, anorexia, nausea, weakness, weight loss, abdominal distention, flatulence, belching, and vomiting. Not a pleasant affair. It is curable with prescribed medication, but you're better off avoiding infection in the first place.

Giardia is spread from the intestines of most mammals such as muskrats, coyotes, deer, beaver, cattle, dogs, cats, and humans. Some can carry and pass on the disease without displaying any symptoms.

All water (including water from springs) should be treated as if it were contaminated. It's critical to treat the water you use for drinking, preparing meals, washing dishes, and brushing teeth, since any of these activities could lead to the ingestion of giardia cysts.

Several methods of water treatment exist, each with advantages and disadvantages. Boiling water kills giardia cysts, but it is time consuming and uses up your fuel supply.

Chloride can be used, but it doesn't kill an equally dangerous protozoa called cryptosporidium. We find that iodine tablets (Portable-Aqua®) are easy-to-use and effective. There's also a whole host of filters on the market which cover the range from filtering large debris to eliminating bacteria, pesticides, and chemicals. Most long-distance hikers who carry filters use the PUR Hiker®.

For a full understanding of waste handling and water-treatment options, we recommend that anyone heading into the woods read *How to Shit in the Woods* by Kathleen Meyer (Ten Speed Press, Berkeley, CA 1994). A vivid title, but the book is packed with valuable information.

I noticed a significant improvement in the trail. Many of the fields and bushy areas looked like they had been mowed or weed-whacked, making for much more pleasant hiking. Thank you, trail maintainers. I eventually found an energy spurt (maybe it was the peas). The easy terrain helped us push on to Ambrose Camp, a three-sided shelter. We pitched our tent in front of the shelter, which meant it would probably be wet with dew in the morning. But we preferred using the tent rather than the open shelter to keep out bugs and mice. Mice and shelters are synonymous. You don't see them until dark. Then you hear them. If you're quick with your flashlight, you'll probably spot several. They're happy to play this game all night. Once, on another hike, a mouse ran across Rich's forehead during the night. I thought it was quite funny but didn't say so at the time. Anyway, Rich still had fun chasing shelter mice with the tent poles. I doubt the mice enjoyed it as much.

We needed more water from the nearby spring. Since we couldn't get the water from the source of the spring, we boiled it and used it for dinner. As the sun went down the temperature dropped rapidly. At 6:45 p.m. we were wearing long pants, socks, long-sleeved turtleneck shirts, fleece jackets, Gore-Tex® rain jackets, and hats. The radio said that we might get frost overnight. It was time to zip our sleeping bags together. Dinner tonight consisted of hot cherry Jell-O® gelatin, hot reconstituted applesauce, and two Lipton dinners. I couldn't wait to finish dinner so we could climb into bed and be warm.

At Peace in the Woods

September 5, Day 24

I was served breakfast in bed this morning. A nice treat! It's so hard to get up when you're toasty warm and comfortable. We lucked out, however, because last night was actually warmer than expected. Today was another beautiful hiking day, but our feet got a soaking from the heavy, early-morning dew. The morning's hike was a mixture of field walks, long stretches over boardwalks, pretty moss and grass-filled streams, a hearty PUD, and tranquil forests.

We passed a grove of wild spreading yews. It always amazes me to see the plants that we buy for landscaping growing in the wild. Last year in the woods along the Appalachian Trail, we saw patches of blue and purple spiderwort—a perennial we pay a lot of money to have in our garden. I guess that everything grows wild somewhere.

We traipsed through some pasture lands and could see cows far in the distance, but the "cow" smell kept growing stronger and stronger. Finally we found ourselves walking through several fields of day-old manure, which made a crunching sound with each footstep. Fortunately, the manure wasn't so fresh that it was wet. The cut remains of the wheat crop were coated with this dry, brown slop. The pungent smell was overpowering, motivating us to hike faster. As the trail exited onto a road, the farmer was turning into the pasture with a fresh load of manure. Rich and I just looked at each other and smiled. We made it out of there just in time, before the "trail" was re-coated. What we thought was a bad experience with dry manure didn't seem all that bad now after seeing the tractor arrive with a new load. It's amazing how quickly our perspectives changed.

On our next road walk, an older gentleman from Torrie Farms was mowing his lawn. We asked him for water, and he filled our bottles with fresh ice water. With all of the cows and manure, I wasn't comfortable using creek water, even iodine treated. The man and Rich chatted awhile near the house while I rested beside the road. We lunched along the next road, just at the entrance to *On Yonder Hills Trails*. It's private land with a network of maintained trails that they open for public hiking and skiing. The sun was nice and warm, but a strong cool breeze was blowing.

The breeze helped as we wandered through fields and forests then began a long slow climb. The nice part was that this section was mowed. I can only imagine the ride down this steep hill on a lawn mower—must be a thrilling ride. The mowed trail continued for a long while as we traversed fields at the top of the hill. Most were newly planted forests and were awash with early autumn color.

We headed down to a lowland and were attacked. As the afternoon warmed, we shed our shirts and became easy game for thousands of hungry mosquitoes. As we hurried along, we flushed about eight ruffed grouse, one by one.

They were close to the trail, so we got a good look at each as it took flight. We've flushed many grouse along the trail, but usually they rush from their perches and fly through the trees. This time they were all nestled in a swamp area with no trees for cover.

Ruffed Grouse

A bird of many names, it is sometimes called a pheasant in the south or a partridge or birch partridge in the north. This brown and gray bird has feathers that form "ruffs" on the sides of the neck, and lower back feathers with small eye spots.

Along the Bruce Trail, we watched them strut slowly across country roads, but usually it's sound not sight that alerts you to a grouse's presence. The first sound is a distinctive drumming or reverberating throb caused by rapidly beating wings. The beats begin slowly and increase in speed for five seconds then turn into a loud hum.

The second sound is the flushing as you get within close range. They wait until you're right next to them, then they fly quickly, often crashing into trees and bushes in their haste to leave.

I felt like I belonged in the woods this afternoon. Hiking in fields of purple asters, with my purple pack, I blended right in. For a long time we walked through a cross-country ski facility. It had wide dirt trails through a mature woods. Even though Rich was only a few feet behind, all I could hear was the wind blowing through the trees—no crack of twigs breaking underfoot, no clang of hiking sticks hitting rocks, no cars, no quarry machines, not even air-planes. I was at peace. It was a joy to walk the mowed paths this afternoon and be one with nature.

Later we found a nesting spot, hidden in a young cedar woods, surrounded by goldenrod and purple aster. The sweet smell enveloped us as we set up camp and prepared dinner.

The Rush to Trail Town
September 6, Day 25

It rained a bit last night, starting at 10 p.m., but didn't last long. We awoke at 6 a.m. to Rich's wrist watch alarm. We had a mission … to make it to the Owen Sound post office before noon. We weren't sure what the post office hours were for Saturday, but we were looking forward to visiting a real trail town with motel, restaurants, and laundry. So we hit the trail at 7 a.m. and scurried along, catching a glimpse of a colorful sunrise. We longed for yesterday's mowed paths as we sloshed through the high grass and weeds. We scared three raccoons up a big, old maple tree. They sat high on a limb peering down at us with their masked, mischievous eyes.

We hiked past the wispy cascade of Ingliss Falls then headed into Owen Sound, driven by the lure of a trail town and all that it has to offer. Along the road, we stuck out our thumbs trying to hitch a ride and avoid the long road walk. Cars and trucks passed us with a wide berth. It was Saturday and everyone had their own agenda from running kids to soccer to picking up something for the yard. Rich got frustrated and decided to stop hitching. I'm less easy to

Ingliss Falls near Owen Sound.

discourage, so I kept trying. After awhile a truck, which had passed us earlier, came back and offered us a ride. As is usually the case, the driver, Bill, had done some backpacking. He drove us to the post office (which would have been a very long walk) and told us stories of bears while on his trip to Alaska.

All our rushing this morning was for naught. The Owen Sound post office wasn't open on Saturdays. So, we'd have to stick around until Monday. Not really a big deal. We were looking forward to some R&R anyway. Bill gave us directions to the Earl Georgas Sports Shop just around the corner that specialized in skiing. The owner had just received a shipment of gaiters, and he had just the right color—purple, a perfect match for my pack and T-shirt. Later, while wandering around Owen Sound, we found additional sporting-goods stores. One covered fishing and hunting while the other specialized in team sports. So, we had found the most appropriate one right off.

Our next concern was where to stay. Rich was in the mood for some privacy rather than being sociable at a bed-and-breakfast. We asked around and found that all of the motels were either up the escarpment along Highways 21 and 6 or on the opposite side of town on Highways 6 and 10. We preferred to stay more centrally located, because we needed the post office on Monday, a drugstore, a laundromat, and restaurants. So we opted for the Brae Briar Bed & Breakfast on the edge of downtown and on the side of town nearer the Bruce Trail. Elizabeth and Don Yule welcomed two smelly hikers graciously. I'm sure they're used to it, but it's sometimes embarrassing, looking your worst and meeting someone for the first time.

First order of business was a shower, slow and warm. Heaven on earth! Then we gathered up all our clothes, except what we wore, and headed up the escarpment to the Westhill Laundromat. Clothes in the washing machine, we went across the street to the Joe Tomatoes restaurant. At noon, Rich ordered a steak dinner and I ordered a pork schnitzel dinner, along with two large beers. Not a scrap was left on our plates when we were done. Back at the laundromat, we met the owner Bob McCulloch who, we could clearly see, enjoys his work. We've become connoisseurs of laundromats from our Appalachian Trail experience. Bob made us feel more welcome than we've ever felt at a laundromat. The cost of washing ($1.75 Canadian) and drying ($0.75 Canadian) included laundry detergent, fabric softener, free coffee, and great conversation. We were actually sorry to see our laundry completed. I'm sure that statement will never again be uttered from these lips.

Now it was time to head downtown. We walked the pier along the harbor, visited the two other sporting goods stores, picked up NewSkin® at a drugstore, and dallied at Tim Horton's over coffee and raisin biscuits. The rest of the afternoon was spent reading, watching TV, and talking to Elizabeth and Don. We walked a few blocks to PizzaPizza for dinner, along the way passing hordes of people fishing on the banks of the Sydenham River. As we ate, a big black cloud passed overhead with thunder, lightning, and rain. Rich quipped, "I wonder how many people are still fishing?" To our amazement, the banks were still lined with fishermen as we made our way back to the B&B. Many had donned rain jackets, but some sat drenched in T-shirts and jeans. A hearty crew for sure.

It rained a lot overnight but we were oblivious to it in our warm, dry bed. In our daily lives, we've become sheltered from the elements as we shuttle from cars to work to homes. Passing rainstorms mean little except a welcome watering for gardens and lawns. When we're on the trail, there's no such escape. Even a short sprinkle means a wet tent (translation = heavier to carry) and wet feet from the shuffle through field grasses and weeds. Rain is a necessity. Without it the stream beds would be dry and water difficult to find, as was true early in our trip. Finding water became an obsession then.

But rain also becomes a nuisance, so we watch each formation of clouds overhead and try to predict the weather. It's much better to have it rain after we've pitched the tent and are snug within. We get far wetter if we have to walk in the rain and pitch the tent while it's still raining. These are things we never even think about in our 20th century insulated lives.

Gourmet Trail Food
September 7, Day 26

Slept late then began the day with a gourmet breakfast. A delicious smell greeted us as we descended the stairs. Elizabeth served a fruit dish that was a work of art, almost too pretty to eat. A wedge of pineapple with its greenery intact and offset peach slices interwoven. Beside it lay wedges of melon and apple with a purple borage flower and mint sprig as garnish. The fruit was followed by a strawberry puff with fresh strawberries, bacon across the top, and a sprinkling of confectioner's sugar. Doused with real maple syrup, it tasted heavenly. The smell that had greeted us was coffee and fresh-baked bread. I piled raspberry jam on a slice of bread and lazily sipped my coffee. It was like a breakfast I'd expect at a very exclusive and expensive hotel, the kind we experienced in our past lives when we traveled as corporate executives. What a trail meal—it sure beat cold toaster pastries and cereal with powdered milk!

Retiring to "the south" seems to be a universal concept, but the exact meaning of "the south" is relative. For U.S. retirees, it generally means Florida or Arizona. For Elizabeth and Don, "the south" meant Owen Sound, Ontario. They had worked in forestry at Long Lac in Terrace Bay, Ontario, far north where temperatures ran at -45°F (-43°C) for three weeks at a time. They found Owen

Gourmet breakfast at Brae Briar Bed and Breakfast.

Sound to be much warmer but with more snow.

We picked a book to read as part of our weekend off. Just as on the trail, we'd take turns reading out loud from a single book. At the bed-and-breakfast, we co-read *Men Are From Mars, Women Are From Venus* by John Gray. Might as well use this downtime to improve our relationship. We decided that we don't fit the male/female stereotypes so we must both be from Pluto.

In the past few days of hiking, we had seen big round white mushrooms, some approaching bowling-ball size. We wondered if they were edible. Elizabeth came into the living room carrying one of these. It was called a puffball and had been given to her by a neighbor. Don fried it with onions, bacon, and butter and gave us each a plate to try. I'm not usually a fan of mushrooms, but this was very good. The fried puffball reminded me of tofu.

Puffball Mushroom

> Puffballs look like large white, meaty balls. They occur alone or in groups in pastures, roadsides, and open spaces in woods in late summer and fall. The ball is attached to the soil by a single thin strand, which breaks away easily at maturity. This mushroom is edible when young and white inside but can be confused with deadly poisonous white Amanitas mushrooms. Therefore, it is best not to eat any wild mushrooms.

It was hard for us to stay stationary and indoors for long,

so we did a self-guided walking tour of the historic homes in Owen Sound and visited the fish ladder. The ladder was a series of ten steps up a channel of raging waters in the Sydenham River and is used by trout in the spring and salmon in the fall to go upstream to reach their spawning grounds. We cheered on the three-foot-long spotted salmon as they fought against seemingly impossible odds to climb the ladder. Fins of some 40 waiting fish cut the water at the base of the ladder, gaining strength and courage to make the attempt. Many failed in their attempted leaps and were swept back down the channel. In the twenty minutes, we spent watching and rooting for them, I saw only one salmon actually make it out the top of the ladder.

From fish to books, our next stop was the Owen Sound library where we spent two hours learning more about things we had seen along the trail. For dinner we visited the Grey Heron restaurant for a full-course meal. Back at the B&B, I soaked in the bathtub complete with bubble bath enjoying every minute of this luxurious break.

A Wonderland of Ferns

September 8, Day 27

First priority this morning was a trip to the post office to pick up our mail drop. Rich went while I washed our dishes and organized things. I couldn't find my blue bandanna. It must be at the laundromat. Rich said that it's a good thing this trail wasn't any longer, or I'd be hiking naked by the end at the rate I was losing things. After sorting the mail drop, we headed downstairs for another gourmet surprise.

The morning's fruit was an arrangement of grapefruit, orange, and kiwi that looked like the petals of a large flower blossom. After the fruit came cheese soufflés puffed high and fluffy, sitting grandly in small white crocks. Beside each soufflé sat a plump sausage and a tomato cut in a saw-tooth pattern also resembling a flower. The tomato was splashed with balsamic vinegar and fresh basil. With two types of fresh-baked bread and coffee, the meal was complete. Though he originally wanted to stay at a motel, Rich conceded that the bed-and-breakfast was a far better choice than a motel would have ever been.

We checked the map and found six miles of road walk heading out of Owen Sound. Yuck! We'd start the day with hot sore feet from pounding the pavement. Don volunteered to drive us to the end of the road walk, and we welcomed the opportunity. On the way we stopped to admire the elk on a farm. There was one large bull with his antlers cut off who bugled at us, but he and his harem of females and young stayed put for our viewing pleasure. Don drove as the road changed from two lanes paved, to two lanes gravel, to one lane gravel, to a dirt farm lane. He stopped when ruts ahead looked impassable. On foot, we were on our way again.

Before we left, Elizabeth gave us a flyer on the many ferns of the Owen Sound area so we spent the morning identifying new ferns. We found bracken, maidenhair spleenwart, bulblet, and northern holly fern. Adding to our list of already identified ferns such as maidenhair, hart's tongue, lady, and New York ferns, we had found eight of the escarpment's 40 possible varieties. We needed to keep looking.

Lady

Northern Holly

Maidenhair
Spleen-wart

Hart's Tongue

Bulblet

New York

Bracken

Maidenhair

Ferns

The Niagara Escarpment along the Bruce Trail is a fantastic place to explore and enjoy the world of ferns. Many of them thrive on the limestone, in the wooded areas on the top, on the face of the cliffs, and in the talus below. The crevices in the exposed bedrock often hold snow and ice well into June and remain cool and wet right through the summer, when the rock above them is hot and dry. Gaze into the crevices, and you'll see lush green mosses and ferns thriving.

There are over 40 varieties of ferns along the Bruce Trail, especially from south of Owen Sound to Tobermory. Some, such as the hart's tongue and wall rue, are rare. Ferns are one of the oldest living organisms on earth. They existed 350 million years ago. The prehistoric fern has been used by archaeologists to determine the age of the layers of the earth.

We walked through cedar forests along the very edge of the escarpment for most of the day with views of a large marsh and open countryside. The soil above the escarpment ranged from a depth of zero to three inches (8 cm). As we crossed north of Township Road, the coverage definitely tended toward the zero end of the scale. Our pace slowed appreciably as we carefully placed each foot. The boulders and slabs of meteorite-like escarpment rock were laced with deep crevices and edged with a fertile grove of poison ivy.

Walking the escarpment rock.

Sue looks eye to eye with her friends the cows.

We quickly put on our gaiters as a shield. We could peer down the crevices some 50 feet (15 m) to the valley below.

I enjoy cows a lot. But, they can be a royal pain when you're looking for water. As we descended the escarpment rocks, we could smell them. After marching through a field with fresh cow plops, we found our cows, in the living flesh, in fields all around us. The map showed three creeks where we might get water for the evening meal. Creek number one was smack dab in a cow pasture. We passed it. Creek number two was a stagnant swamp. We passed it. Creek number three was bone dry. Now what? On a stretch of road, we passed a few, very-spread-out houses, but no one was home. We walked on, hoping against hope that there'd be some more houses. A truck came along. Rich flagged it down and asked the driver if he knew where we could get water. They worked out a plan: We'd give the driver our three empty bottles, and he'd drive to his house, fill them with water, and meet us up the road at a large pile of harvested logs. We hiked to the logs, took off our packs, and waited next to the sign that declared this to be the corner of Coles Sideroad and Taylor Sideroad. Within five minutes, the truck and driver returned. The driver's name was Ken Taylor. He brought our filled bottles and also two frozen sports bottles of water. He said that he takes the frozen bottles out on the tractor so he can have a refreshing cold drink during the day. It was a very thoughtful gesture, and we thanked Ken but declined the frozen water. We talked for a while about the harvesting of forests, then Ken drove back down his family's namesake sideroad and we continued hiking up Coles Sideroad.

Waiting for water on the log pile at Taylor Sideroad.

A Side Trip to Bruce Caves

September 9, Day 28

Last night we were lulled to sleep by the hooting of a great horned owl. Its nest must have been in the large maple tree which provided a canopy for our tent. Every few minutes it would give a soft, soothing call. About midnight the owl moved to the other side of the field by another tree line to hunt. We couldn't have had a more relaxing sleep that night.

We headed up through recently harvested woods. The dirt road was filled with deep ruts, but fortunately it was dry allowing us to pick our way along. We passed a field having hundreds of sheep that were beginning to grow their winter coats. Some were still huddled in groups sleeping. They roused themselves and baahed as we passed.

Then we had beautiful views along Skinner's Bluff. We could see three islands and a lone sailboat on the azure water of Colpoy's Bay far below. If it had been warmer, we would have felt like we were in the Caribbean. Across the bay were the long stretches of white cliffs called Colpoy's Bluff. In a day or two, we would be on them. The clouds rolled in and turned the sparkling blue waters to a dull gray.

The trail directed us back into the woods anyway, so the cloud cover didn't matter.

I talked Rich into taking a little side trail to a place on the map labeled "Bruce Caves." The trail guide gave no description, so we didn't know quite what to expect. As we headed downhill, I hoped this wasn't a busy tourist trap. We quickly reached an empty gravel parking area. To the left was a small picnic pavilion and outhouses. To the right was a sign stating "Bruce Caves Trail—Steep and Rocky." No one else was around. We headed to the right and followed a spattering of rocks in a dirt path for what seemed like a long time. Actually, on the way back, I timed it and it was all of five minutes. Funny how your perception shifts when you're anticipating something. Like when you're young and waiting for Christmas, it takes forever to arrive.

We did reach the caves and, as promised, the trail did become rocky and mildly steep. The caves were great—tall, wide caverns carved into the escarpment rock by ancient seas. We looked around inside but didn't stay too long. It looked like rock regularly broke off from the cave ceiling. Another cave was formed from a huge chunk of rock that sheered off, falling back toward the main escarpment. It was hard to envision how that happened. One cave had a pillar of rock in the middle and several holes big enough for a human to crawl through. We agreed that we were glad we had made the side trip.

Then came a short hike to Island View Drive where we stuck out our thumbs hoping for a ride into Wiarton. Cars were few and far between. Probably 20 passed, each giving us a wide berth, until finally Bruce McGill stopped. Bruce

Sue peering into the hugh limestone cavern of Bruce Caves.

was a Physical Education teacher at Wiarton and was running school errands during a non-class period. He brought us directly to the post office.

Rich went in and picked up our package. The postman knew exactly where the box was and said, "Hey, you're early," because we arrived before the expected-arrival date that I had written on the box.

We headed to the bay and checked into the Bluewater Tent and Trailer Park. For $16 we got to pitch our tent and take showers. It's our first campsite on the bay. We're definitely outnumbered by trailers. I'd say 40 to 1.

After showers, we walked the one block back into town for dinner, ice cream, and an hour of reading at the town library. Wiarton was a nice trail town. It had everything that a long-distance hiker needs—lodging, restaurants, post office, laundry, and drugstore, all within a walkable area.

When we returned to our tent site, we had neighbors. The section of campground that we set up in was ours alone when we moved into our assigned site. Now there were an additional 10 trailers. We greeted one of our neighbors and were greeted back by a terse, "Are you always in the habit of stealing campsites?" Taken aback, we weren't quite sure what to make of this guy. Come to find out, he was here for a week teaching wood carving and had left some stuff on the picnic table to "reserve" his spot. We had ignored the stuff on the picnic table assuming someone had forgotten it, because the lady at check-in had told us that no one was in this whole section. Our angry neighbor had never officially checked in. Anyway, later in the evening he apologized to us. Everyone else around here had been very friendly.

Big Two-mile Day
Sept. 10, Day 29

The rain began at 3 a.m. At 7 a.m. it was still raining, with the temperature around 55°F (13°C), so we donned our rainjackets and headed to a diner for breakfast.

Over breakfast we discussed what we should do. Part of the decision process included when we would arrive at our next mail drop in Lion's Head. Arriving on a Saturday or Sunday would only mean staying over until Monday. Since we had to slow up anyhow, it didn't much matter where we slowed up—it might as well be here, and we could avoid hiking in the rain. Our ornery neighbor wanted our camp-site, so we had to pack up one way or another. One option was to check into a B&B in Wiarton and spend the day at the library. Other than that, we didn't see many choices of things to do around town. Another option was to pack up and hike on. There were other bail-out possibilities along our route in case the weather got ugly.

Back at the tent, the rain had dwindled to a slight drizzle, the wind was light, and it was fairly warm. We packed up and decided to hike on. We followed the blazes through Bluewater Park to the waterworks road. After the water fil-tration plant, the road turned into a path of small rocks right along the shore of Colpoy's Bay. Shoreline trees sheltered us from the breeze, and we warmed up as we hiked on enjoying the rough, wind blown seas along the shore. After a quarter mile, the Bruce Trail turned left away from the water and ascended the escarpment, first on stone steps then via a metal spiral staircase as the escarpment rock face became vertical. The path at the top of the escarpment led directly to the "Corran," an old stone mansion now in ruins. We followed the blazes from Wiarton, but the map didn't look anything like the blazed trail. The map indicated that we would be at the top, following the escarpment, yet we were heading away from it. The landowner may have revoked permission for the trail to cross his land, because the next thing we knew, we were marching north along Highway 6. Cars zipped by us throwing up a cloud of cold spray on our left. The wind and rain had picked up pummeling us sideways on our right. A walk through the woods in light rain can be pleasant. A road walk in the wind-driven

Walking the shoreline along Colpoy's Bay.

rain is not as appealing.

As we inched along the highway, a sign caught Rich's eye. He has much better long-distance vision than I do. It said "Glen Miller Motel, $40 double includes continental breakfast." It only took a quick glance at one another to decide. We sloshed in and were greeted warmly by the owners, Fred and Loreena Richardson. Fred told us to help ourselves to the remaining coffee and food from today's breakfast, and Loreena volunteered to toss our wet clothing into her dryer.

In our travels, we have found that there is little correlation between the price of lodging and meals, and the quality and service provided. Here on the lower end of the cost spectrum was the best in service and friendliness and great lodging. The room was spacious, clean, and nicely decorated. There was a separate, very comfortable sunroom for the continental breakfast. As the rain and wind continued to intensify, we were ever so glad that we had stopped even if it meant we only did a 2-mile (3 km) day. A lazy day of reading and watching TV felt good. However, we knew we were becoming bored when Rich began noticing the differences between toilets. For those of you who must know, the drain hole in this toilet was in the front whereas most toilets have drain holes in the back.

Where'd the Water Go?

Sept. 11, Day 30

With trepidation we headed out into another day of drizzle after a breakfast of cereal, toast and jelly, orange juice, coffee, and bananas. Were we making the right decision? The forecast still didn't sound good. But we had miles to make, and it was hard to sit still. Off we went praying the day would be kind to us. We veered off the road into a cow pasture and thought maybe this was a mistake, as we sloshed through wet grass and flooded sections of pasture. A farmer came across the field in his pick-up truck, bringing hay to his beef cows. We talked for a bit and thanked him for letting the trail cross his land. In his pasture, we saw a rushing creek slip down a crack in solid rock and disappear. This area, known as a karst, was a sight we would see again later in the day.

The trail took us along the top edge of the escarpment overlooking Colpoy's Bay. It was rough going, and we slid regularly on the moss-covered rocks, trying to dodge the patches of poison ivy. The view across the bay was of the cliffs that we had walked a few days ago, muted and serene. The gray sky melted into the gray bay.

Our luck held and it only sprinkled on us periodically. Of course, that was when we stopped for a break or for lunch. This meant we could only grab a handful of food and move on, not take the restful break that we normally require each day. By 2:30 p.m. we dragged ourselves into the Cape Croker Park General Store and relished the feel of a chair beneath us as we downed cheeseburgers, fries, and coffee. Not exactly the perfect nutrition for a hiker's needs, but, it gave me a second wind for a few hours. Then when I began to tire again, Rich suggested listening to the radio. He had already tuned it to a rock-and-roll station, which boosted my spirits as I marched to the quick beat of the songs.

Many days we hiked in silence with an occasional shout of "P.I.," short for poison ivy. We said it so many times each day to warn each other that we felt the need to abbreviate it. If it was just in small patches, we gingerly tiptoed through. But if it grew into the path and stood a foot tall, we stopped to put on our knee-high gaiters.

After Cape Croker Park, the top of the escarpment meta-morphosed to a different animal. Still forested with birches and maples, it roared rather then purred. First we had to climb up on all fours to scale the boulders, then we had to use a ladder to climb the last vertical section. The walk along the top edge was cushy with topsoil rather than bare rock—a treat to the feet. But, to our great surprise it wasn't flat. In fact, it was quite hilly, and we broke a sweat climbing up and down despite the natural air conditioning of the slight drizzle, which tried to keep us cool.

For the first time we camped alongside the trail. The terrain was quite rocky, and this was one of the few flat spots that we saw as we marched along. The drizzle had turned into a light shower, so we decided to make camp before it picked up any more strength. We felt confident that no one would be out strolling on the trail on this cool, rainy, Thursday night.

Never assume anything by it's appearance alone. Many times you will arrive at the wrong conclusion.

Ignore that Grumbling Man Behind You
September 12, Day 31

Neither of us was anxious to leap out of bed this morning. We could tell it was not a stellar, blue-sky day. The rain had stopped, but the saturated woods continued to drip on us, especially when the wind blew. Even worse, the mosquitoes were out in force. Rich lured me on saying, "One hour to the next general store." With visions of good stuff to eat, we headed out over the slippery rock trail. The low bushes covering the forest floor had turned yellow, helping to brighten the dreary morning.

We came off this section of escarpment the same way we got on it—straight down the rock cliff. We tossed our sticks below to free our hands. By 7:30 a.m. we were on a nice easy dirt-road walk around the end of Hope Bay, past a peaceful community of cottages. Then disappointment. The Cedarholme General Store didn't open until 9 a.m. Drats! We could have waited but didn't want to give up an hour and a half of morning walk. We filled our water bottles from the side spigot and moved on, replacing visions of food with visions of glacial potholes.

We didn't really know what to expect of the potholes. The

guidebook said that they were formed by granite rocks getting caught in a depression of the softer limestone rock as the glacial waters receded. The swirling granite carved out an area of the limestone. We pictured a bowl-type affair. What we saw were several deep circular holes in the escarpment rock, probably three feet (1 m) in diameter. One was ten feet (3 m) deep, straight down. It was as if a giant auger had drilled into the rock. The power of water and time is truly amazing.

The path out of Hope Bay had been slow and gradual. But all that changed as we reached the top of the escarpment. Once again we were in mountains, and the hiking became very slow. We put on our gaiters to fend off the poison ivy, and even though the temperature was only in the low 60s (16°C), Rich took off his shirt. It seemed like forever before we reached the first lookout. By the time we did, Rich was dripping in sweat. After several lookouts, the gray skies parted temporarily to let the sun through, twinkling off the waters below turning them to an azure hue. Groups of loons fished in the water far below, their distant songs echoing off the cliffs.

Reaching Bruce County Road 9, we hoped to hitch a ride. The trail guide said that County Road 9 was a busy road, but at noon on Friday, past tourist season, few cars went by. Finally a truck stopped. A fisherman was taking his catch to Lion's Head. Contrary to our usual habit of sitting in back, Rich sat inside the cab, and I climbed into the bed of the truck with two large bins of fresh fish. The floor was wet with sloshing fish water, so I had to squat rather than sit during the ride. We were very glad that we got picked up though, it would have been a long road walk. The fisherman even offered Rich a free fish, but we had no way to carry or cook it. We thanked him but declined the offer. Next on the trail was a trek around Lion's Head peninsula. The guidebook said that this area had spectacular views, so we hiked on looking forward to exploring more unknown territory.

We stopped for lunch shortly after the truck let us off, and it started to drizzle. Rich was none too happy. Once again we cut lunch short. Why did it rain each time we tried to eat lunch? The initial part of the walk north from County Road 9 was on a gravel road. When the road ended, we found ourselves knee deep in poison ivy. Rich said, "That's it! We're turning around and hitching into Lion's Head." I just remained quiet and let him grumble.

I was apprehensive about hiking into the Lion's Head peninsula, too, but I couldn't tell Rich, or he'd turn back for sure. The top of the escarpment since Cape Croker had been downright mountainous. If this section was, too, we'd be in for a long, tough eight miles (13 km) and maybe not make it to the Lion's Head post office by noon on Saturday. So we trudged on in silence. I was pleasantly surprised. The terrain was difficult but not mountainous. By the time we reached the cliffs at the northwest corner of the peninsula, we were both having a good time. The trail followed right along the edge of the cliff with drop-offs below us of 175 feet (53 m). Sometimes we were rather nervous about stepping on rocks that appeared to be cracking away from the mainland or that were overhangs with no support below. The trail boldly went on. We watched each footstep care-

The edge of the escarpment along Lion's Head peninsula.

fully. It would lead right to the cliff edge and then make an abrupt turn back toward the woods. Time after time a beautiful view was presented to us. Sometimes we would inch out to look over, straight down into the tops of trees far below, noticing that we were on an overhang. Even though we knew that the rock had hung like that for hundreds of years, we didn't linger.

By 4:30 p.m. we had wound our way down off the cliff to McKay's Harbor campsite. What a treat! Our own private beach and camping area. We selected a tent site up a little from the beach in a grove of cedar trees and set up camp. I don't know the official criteria for membership in the polar bear club, but as far as I was concerned, we qualified that night as we skinny dipped in Georgian Bay. We didn't stay in the water long, just long enough to wash away the grime and sweat. As we rinsed off, our voices gained an octave. Rich's was particularly high. Boy, was it cold!

We immediately started our evening meal, feasting on hot peach Jell-O® gelatin, applesauce, and Lipton chicken-and-rice dinner while listening to the sound of waves lapping on the beach. A flock of loons played offshore, serenading us with their distinctive calls. We passed the 45th parallel today which meant that we were equidistant between the equator and the north pole, although the temperature sure felt like we were closer to the north pole.

A Double-swim Day
September 13, Day 32

Rich's watch alarm beeped at 6 a.m. It was still dark, and we peeked outside the tent to see a glimmer of orange sun rising above the bay. Rich wisely decided that we should sleep a little longer, partly due to my grumbles and partly due to the darkness outside. So we ate our Pop Tarts® pastries and snuggled back for another doze. He rousted me again around 6:30 a.m. By now the horizon was a full-width blaze of orange and pink, and we could see the world around us. So off we went with trail town on our minds.

The walk along the west side of the Lion's Head peninsula was so much easier than the east side had been—or maybe we just had more energy now. At one point, Rich teased me by going off the trail in a loop just to see if I'd follow him. I passed the alertness test and said, "Hey, where are you going? The trail's over there." Rich must have felt I needed a test, because a half hour into our hike, I realized that we hadn't had any cereal for breakfast.

By 9 a.m. we were in Lion's Head. We picked up our mail drop at the post office and headed to the Village Restaurant for a real breakfast. We were trying to decide what to do. The sun was out for the first time in three days, and it seem a shame to spend this great day in town. After a good meal, all I really wanted was to do laundry (since we had bathed in the bay last night). We asked around and found there wasn't a laundromat in Lion's Head.

As we ate, we studied the maps. Only three more days of hiking until the end ... it had gone by so fast! Two women walked up to our breakfast table. They were Laura from London, England, and Nancy from Toronto. We had met them on the Lion's Head loop yesterday afternoon and were worried about them making it back to their car before dark. We were very glad to see that they had made it. In talking about where we had come from and were we were going, we lamented that there was another long road walk out of Lion's Head. They volunteered to drive us. So, we finished breakfast quickly. Rich filled our water bottles and ran next door to buy batteries for my flashlight. I paid the food bill and dashed across the street to make a quick phone call home. Stuffing the mail drop food in our packs, we were on our way again. Laura and Nancy took us around Lion's Head Bay and dropped us off where the trail headed into the woods.

With an easy hike in, we were at Reed's Dump by 11:30 a.m. Reed's Dump is such an odd name. To me it conjured images of someone's garbage dump, and I couldn't imagine why it would make a good campsite. What we found was a level area along the escarpment face which was treed but cleared for camping and with a short path down to a white cobblestone beach. At first we toyed with the idea of staying here overnight but that, too, seemed like a waste of a perfectly good afternoon of hiking. So we decided to do laundry, eat lunch, and head north. Doing laundry consisted of stripping naked and rinsing our clothes in the bay then laying them on the white pebble beach to dry. While we were at it, we went for another swim. Though the water was cold, we lingered a long time. Having the sun out made a world of difference. Three sailboats were playing directly offshore from us. If they had binoculars, I'm sure they got quite a show. So be it. We couldn't resist the opportunity to get clean.

Dump

Some of the coves at the base of the escarpment along Georgian Bay contain cobblestone beaches. The cobblestones were formed by glacial and post-glacial wave action.

The beaches have intriguing names such as High Dump, Halfway Dump, and Coony's Dump. The names date back to the 19th century when logging was the main industry of the area. Logs were cut inland through the winter months and then dumped into Georgian Bay. From there boats would tow them to a local sawmill.

We hiked three more miles (4.8 km) to the beach below Smoky Head. Smoky Head was a great lookout from a ledge on the cliff. Below us curved white pebble beaches and azure sea, ending at a point of land called Cape Chin. The descent off the escarpment was gradual, and just before the beach we found a nice campsite nestled in a grove of cedar. It became home. At 3:30 p.m. we set up camp and walked down to the beach. Spreading our hiking clothes on the white rocks in the sun to dry, we went swimming once again. This time we could really swim, the placid water dropped to a swimable depth very quickly.

This unique beach was comprised totally of flat white rocks with rounded edges. The rocks ranged from pebble-size to four inches (10 cm) in diameter and were piled in waves parallel to the sea, sculpted by previous wave action. We used the curved furrows as a comfortable chaise lounge and relaxed while loons played on the sea in front of us.

Lounging on a natural cobblestone chaise lounge.

Where the Heck Are We?

September 14, Day 32

Dinner last night was an uninspiring event. We reconstituted spaghetti sauce, tossed in some olive oil, and boiled spaghetti. I had aliquoted olive oil into small shampoo bottles—the type you get at hotels. In this case, I must not have washed the bottle thoroughly enough. Our spaghetti dinner tasted of soap, and we joked about being able to blow bubbles.

When morning arrived, our world was shrouded in fog with a heavy dew. It was a treat to put on dry clothes, although they still smelled, but only a little. We walked the beach for a short while then headed into the woods. As we walked, the canopy above dripped water on us. Though not far from the escarpment edge, we passed through a large swamp. There were trees recently felled by beaver, and we scared up 20 ducks from their Sunday morning reverie on the water. I enjoyed the stiles in this section. Rather than ladder-like affairs, they were stairs that were easy to climb up and down, even for uncoordinated people like me.

The trail brought us back out to overhanging ledges as we approached Devils' Monument. Neither of us felt comfortable standing on these rock ledges, so we scampered over them. Devil's Monument was a free-standing flowerpot, but the view of it was slightly impeded by the trees that have grown on and around it. Shortly after Devil's Monument, the trail began a long road walk. At first it was on a low-use, gravel road, but when it turned into a paved road, we stuck out our thumbs. Tom Cox stopped to pick us up. He was from East Lansing, Michigan, and was in the area camping and hiking. His backseat and trunk were already filled with camping gear. So we set our packs on top of the open trunk, and all of us squeezed into the frontseat. At first we asked Tom to drive us two miles (3 km) down the road to Larkwhistle, an award-winning perennial garden which had been recommended to us. It was supposedly open weekends in the fall, and this was a Sunday afternoon. But, on the fence sat a "closed for the season" sign, so Tom drove on. He took us a total of three miles (5 km) and left us at the corner of Gillies Lake Road and a gravel side road. As a farewell gift, he gave us each a maple leaf made of maple sugar, which we devoured within seconds of him leaving.

We walked the sideroad past a big swamp as it gradually turned into two gravel tracks with a grass center. With each footstep, frogs of all sizes leaped for cover. Since Rich and I were walking side by side, it often meant that frogs were leaping in front of the other person, and we had to tread carefully to avoid stepping on them.

Upon entering the Bruce Peninsula National Park, we felt like we were in the twilight zone. The two-lane dirt path continued for awhile then transformed into a wide snowmobile path (complete with warning signs) then into a hiking trail. The sign at the entrance indicated seven km (4 miles) to High Dump. Once we passed that sign, we hadn't a clue as to where we were until four miles (7 km) later when we saw another sign for High Dump. The trail must have been rerouted, because it didn't resemble the map or trail guide. We had planned to get water at Crane River, but we never passed it. We never saw any blue-blazed side trails, including one that was supposed to lead to a hand pump for water. At least we knew for sure that if we kept going, High Dump would have water (from Georgian Bay). Around 5:00 p.m. we saw the sign for High Dump. We covered 23 miles (37 km) today and actually hiked 20 miles (32 km). That's a long day for us, and we arrived tired. First order of business was a swim. The late afternoon sun would set soon. So before setting up camp, we grabbed dry clothes and headed down to the water. The swim was cold and quick, but we always sleep much better when the sweat is rinsed off. We spread our clothes on the white-rock beach to dry, catching the last few rays of sun.

The trek today had its rewards. Several times, grouse strutted across the path in front of us, oblivious to our presence. Then, in the late afternoon, while Rich had his headphones on listening for the weather report, the silence was broken by a loud rattle. We both heard it and jumped back. We could tell the rattling came from the left side and since it was a wide path, Rich dashed by on the far right. Sticking its head out onto the path was a Massassauga rattlesnake, about ¾ of an inch (1.9 cm) in width. It was trying to cross the path, and we got in its way. It stopped rattling, so I dashed by on the far right just as Rich had. We watched it for a few minutes, and it didn't move; so we continued down the trail, leaving it to cross in peace.

Eastern Massassauga Rattlesnake

This snake is a shy fellow who would prefer to avoid your company. The rattle is often used to alert you to its presence. Unfortunately, human development has encroached on its preferred habitat, and an attitude of "the only good snake is a dead snake" has lead to its decline. The small, 18 to 28 inches (46 to 71 cm), elusive snake has a mildly venomous bite usually not fatal to humans. It can be found in areas north of Lake Erie, east of Lake Huron, the entire Bruce Peninsula, and around the Georgian Bay coast.

The snake is gray to light brown with rows of dark gray, brown, or black spots. It is stocky with a short, small but well developed rattle. The Massassauga rattler eats warm-blooded prey, primarily voles and deer mice. In spring and fall, it is more diurnal in its habits and often basks or actively forages during the day. When daytime temperatures become too warm in summer, it shifts to a nocturnal schedule. It is also an accomplished swimmer.

The Eastern Massassauga rattlesnake was placed on the Canadian Endangered Species list as a threatened species in 1990 and is protected by law. Penalties are stiff for killing a rattlesnake, so if you see or hear one, step lightly and walk away.

Observers of the Fall Migration

September 15, Day 33

Slept in this morning—we earned it! We were surprised yesterday by the steep descent to High Dump campground. Previous descents to dumps had been gradual. As a result, first thing this morning, before I was alert, I had to climb straight up a rugged rock cliff. The overcast skies and a nice breeze actually made for pleasant hiking along the cliff edge where often there's no tree cover. The two islands that we could see last night (Flowerpot and Bear's Rump Islands) were lost in fog this morning. Our gentle country lane stroll of yesterday was gone too. The trail guide said that today's hike would be the most difficult part of the trail, and sure enough, the terrain was hilly with rough, slippery escarpment rock.

We had a visitor last night. Most nights we hung all of the food including toothpaste and pots. But last night, we came up with a thousand excuses not to do it. It was getting dark. I couldn't find the rope. None of the branches was low enough. The bag would get wet if it rained, and so on. Something kept sniffing at the tent corner where we stored the food bag. We shooed it away several times, and in the

Walking the cobblestone beaches along Georgian Bay.

morning everything was still intact. We thought that it was a porcupine, but we found out later that we were in black bear country. I'm glad that Rich didn't unzip the tent fly to look out. And if it was a bear, I'm also glad that he or she was not very hungry. Not hanging our food bag was a mistake we won't make again.

As we picked our way through the rocks, we came to the escarpment edge many times. Gradually the fog lifted, the shadow of islands appeared, and we watched Cave Point take shape as we got closer. I couldn't resist taking pictures of the spectacular cliffs from our break spot along Halfway Dump. Within an hour, we were standing on top of the cliff that I had just taken a picture of from the beach. The rocks were wet and slippery, appearing to sweat. We continued along and lunched on the beach at the Ledges.

On top of the escarpment cliffs along Georgian Bay.

As we sat on a rock ledge eating, a flock of Canada geese came toward us. They were flying just above water level, as they crossed Georgian Bay on their migration south. Now with the cliffs in front of them, they flapped hard. They banked upward to clear the trees onshore and flew fifteen feet (5 m) over our heads. They were working hard, tired after a long flight over water. Last night, even after dark, and throughout the day, waves of migrating Canada geese flew overhead, possibly taking advantage of the prevailing northerly winds. Winter can't be too far behind.

We were on beaches repeatedly today but never swam. The breeze and cool temperatures kept us out of the water. As we progressed north along the stone beaches, the rounded cobblestones got larger then turned into jagged rocks. They were very hard to walk on, providing an unstable footing. In fact, all of today was tough walking, and when we stopped at 4:30 p.m., we were just as tired as yesterday even though we did only half as many miles. Part of our slowness was because we were sightseeing. We stopped often to enjoy the views, glance at caves, grottoes, and all of the exotic things along the way. The Cyprus Lake area was especially scenic. There were many people on this section of trail doing a one-day exploration.

A natural stone bridge in the Cyprus Lake area.

Success at Last
September 16, Day 35

We got an early start today in anticipation of completing our journey. The northerly winds were brisk, bashing waves against the shore as we carefully walked by, awed by the power of water. Our views were crystal clear—Bear's Rump Island and all of its little brothers and sisters were visible on the horizon. From Dunk's Bay, we could even see the flowerpot on the end of Flowerpot Island towering 50-foot (15 m) in the air. Along the shore, the crashing waves rang in our ears, but if we turned inland 20 feet (6 m), only woods sounds surrounded us.

The white blazes led us directly to the shoreline at Dunk's Bay. Waves crashed upon the jagged shore and drenched the rocks where we were supposed to walk. At one point, a rock promontory jutted out, and we needed to edge around in front of it between the bulging rock and the teeming waters a few feet below. A slip would send us into the deep, cold waves. With a backpack strapped on, we figured we'd go down like a rock. The finish line was so close, and this was no way to end our hike. We backtracked and opted for the foul-weather path just inside the tree line.

Our feet flew over the last few miles, drawn not only by the lure of trail town but by the pleasure of reaching a goal.

We walked hand in hand to touch the final cairn on Little Tub Harbor in Tobermory. It had taken us five weeks to walk end to end.

The northern terminal cairn on Little Tub Harbor in Tobermory.

Still, our adventure was not over. At this point, we had no idea how we were going to get home. We've learned on other hikes to flow with nature and things will work out. On the Appalachian Trail, it was an initial struggle to give up control, to realize that we couldn't be in control and to accept that as OK. In fact, this is one of the great lessons that long-distance hiking has taught us. We enter hikes prepared to deal with extremes of temperature, time, and moisture, but we no longer try to control them. Our experience has shown time and again that if you're in need, help will arrive. It's best not to over plan, stick to a schedule, or try to maintain control like we attempt to do in our civilized lives.

We asked about lodgings around Tobermory and found a good deal with off-season rates at the Peacock Villa Motel. We checked in and immediately took showers. I stopped at a pay phone and left a message on my cousins' recorder letting them know that we had arrived safely in Tobermory. Next stop was the laundromat. While our clothes washed, we went across the street for fish-and-chips dinners. At each place we went, we asked about potential transportation. The motel owner told us that a bus ran a few times a week during summer but had stopped for the winter. He suggested that a seniors' group was heading toward Toronto on a bus trip tomorrow, and they might let us tag along if they had room. We had a nice conversation about hiking with a couple in the restaurant. They volunteered to drive us anywhere around Tobermory that we might need to go, but they had to head back to Michigan that same afternoon, the opposite direction from where we were going.

Back to the laundromat to dry our clothes, then we dropped them off at the motel. On our door was a note. My parents had called saying that they were on their way north to pick us up. As it turned out, we were ahead of the rough schedule I had put together. My parents, who had been living at our house while we were gone, were going (in a round-about way) toward Florida on September 15th. They happened to be at my cousins' house in Stoney Creek when I left the message. So they drove our van, which we had left at my cousins', to Tobermory, gathered us up, and drove sx hours back down to Stoney Creek. A mother's love sure runs deep!

Re-entry (and beyond)
Day 36

*J*ust as we had to slowly build endurance when we began this adventure, re-entry to a normal life needs to be gradual after a long-distance hike. We had just spent weeks in quiet solitude moving to the rhythms of nature. The adjustment back to the noises, lights, and demands of life in today's society was jarring. The sun would set and our bodies would be ready for bed even if it was only 7 p.m. The distance we covered in five weeks of walking flashed by in six hours of driving. At home the mail had piled up, and people waited in line to hear our glorious tales. Overwhelmed, we wanted to crawl back to the woods. It was a normal reaction. We had been there before and knew that we just needed to take things one at a time and allow ourselves to adjust slowly.

Equipment

$\mathcal{H}$aving the right equipment can make or break a back-packing trip. The trick is to carry as little as possible and to keep your pack weight as low as possible, but still meet your basic needs and be able to adjust to the swings in temperature and moisture. We fine-tuned and adjusted what we carried on our 2,200-mile Appalachian Trail journey. Still, setting out on a new adventure, we found ourselves packing too much and discarding or mailing home unneeded "stuff" early in the trip. The early miles on the Appalachian Trail were littered with all sorts of necessities that people decided were no longer necessary. We are accustomed to many conveniences in modern life and think that we can't live without some of them. But, as the miles accumulate under our feet, the pack pulls on our shoulders, and the soles of our feet begin to hurt from the pounding, we find that in reality we can live much more comfortably with fewer things.

So here, rightly or wrongly, is what we carried on the Bruce Trail. It worked for us and with modifications, might work for you also.

Packs:

$\mathcal{W}$e swear by our Dana Designs internal frame packs. Rich has an Arcflex Alpine®. Mine is an Arclight Glacier®. Each holds about 5,000 cubic inches of gear. It can be annoying to have to unpack your whole load to reach something at the bottom of the single compartment, but the comfort of these packs is far superior to any external-frame packs that we've ever carried. The packs mold to your back and bear the weight snugly on your hips. We each carry two diaper pins attached to the outside of our packs. We use them to hang socks and shirts on our pack for drying and for emergency repair of anything. The locking mechanism on diaper pins is much better than on safety pins. Snag a sock on an overhanging branch as you duck under it, and a safety pin breaks open while the diaper pin holds fast.

We purchased small wet/dry packs for our Dana Designs packs. These are pouches that attach to the front of the pack and cross your belly. The wet part holds a Nalgene® bottle for easy, rapid access to drinking water without stopping. The dry part is a zippered pouch in which we carry maps, trail munchies, camera, and sit-upons (see Tyvek®); the things we need ready access to. Our camera is a small, lightweight Pentax UC-1®, which handles the light range needed for exposing slide film. It looks like it's survived a long, hard life, but it has served us well for 2,700 trail miles. Rich, being a photographer, misses having extra lenses and a tripod. But, we can't justify the weight that they would add.

Attached to the back of my pack is a trusty plastic trowel, which we use to dig six-inch holes for pit stops. It also houses my whistle and has duct tape wrapped around the handle. We figured the poop shovel was a good home for the whistle. When you set off to use the shovel is the time that you leave your pack behind and venture off the trail, a perfect opportunity to get lost. Blow the whistle so your companion can find you. Plastic is lightweight but expect the trowel to break easily. Ours is a stubby version of its former svelte self. A metal trowel would last longer and dig holes better, but it would also add weight to your pack. There's always a trade off. The duct tape around the trowel handle softens the grip and comes in handy for any type of repair. We've used it to bandage feet, mend a tent hole, tape a torn map together, etc.

Tent:

We shopped long and hard and evaluated many tents before ending up with our NorthFace Ventilator®. It is long enough for Rich's six-foot length (many tents aren't), has a fly which comes low enough to the ground to keep rain splashes out, and fits two of us comfortably. Plus we can sit up in it to change clothes and store our packs in the vestibule. In addition, it weighs only 4 pounds, 4 ounces (1.9 kg). After seven months of trail, and four hurricanes, it was and continues to be a good choice. We carry only four tent stakes and leave the stuff bag, guy strings, and other tent stakes at home.

Tyvek®:

Tyvek® is a moisture-barrier material that is used as a house wrap in home building. Cut slightly smaller than the shape of your tent floor, it makes the perfect ground cover. It's lightweight and puts up with the abuse of multiple foldings and unfoldings. Our sit-upons (which, as the name implies, we sit on to keep our butts clean and dry) are also scrap squares of Tyvek®. You can buy large rolls of Tyvek® at a hardware/home building store or check with a local builder for a small piece.

Sleeping Bags:

Mummy bags are the only way to reduce weight and ensure warmth. You have a choice synthetic or down. Down is lighter but is useless when wet. We opted for Wiggy's synthetic bags to assure warmth when wet. We don't have to hassle with keeping the bags in an extra plastic bag. We simply pack them in their compression sacks and put them in the sleeping bag compartment at the bottom of the packs without worry.

Rain Gear:

If it rains enough you'll get wet. That's a fact of life. The trouble is if you try to stay one-hundred-percent dry, you'll get soaked from sweat. So you need to find a balance. We love our Dana Designs pack covers. They come with built-in hoods and can be tied across your chest to cover your shoulders. They keep you dry and sweat-free in everything except rain being driven sideways or straight at your belly by wind. These pack covers work over any manufacturer's internal frame packs.

We carry Gore-Tex® rain jackets from LL Bean for extra-heavy protection from cold rain and wind. For the Bruce

Trail, we also had OR (Outdoor Research) crushable wide-brimmed hats to keep off the sun and rain.

Gaiters:

*G*aiters are bands made of nylon or Gore-Tex® material that wrap around your legs and fasten with hook-and-loop closures (such as Velcro®). They're often used by cross-country skiers to keep snow out of boots. Hikers use gaiters in short versions to keep stones and dirt out of their boots. We use tall (knee-high) Gore-Tex® gaiters for the above reason plus to avoid poison ivy, to keep water out of our boots, and as a warm layer in cold and rain.

Boots:

*C*arrying a heavy backpack over rough terrain requires substantial boots. But again, it's important to keep weight as low as possible. We both wear all-leather boots by One Sport. The specific model is the Morraine®. They have Vibram® soles to grip on slippery surfaces, good ankle support, and all-leather construction to help keep water out. It's critical to get boots that are comfortable and big enough. As you hike, your feet will swell both in width and length. On our six-month Appalachian Trail hike, our feet grew one-half to a full shoe size permanently.

Inside the boots, we wear a flat Spenco® insole and on top of that a Spenco® arch-support insole. The insoles that come from the boot manufacturer are for looks only and provide no support. Your feet will take a pounding and need the cushioning that insoles provide. Less expensive insoles compress rapidly and soon become useless. To ensure that you get the right size, lay the insole on the floor and stand on it with your socks on. Make sure that it is not only long enough, but wide enough.

When buying boots, wear the socks you will hike in (see Socks section) and take insoles. Go boot shopping in the evening. Your feet will have swelled from a day of standing or walking just like they will on the trail. You need to find boots that have room to spare and are comfortable when wearing both the insoles and the hiking socks.

On this hike, I was constantly nursing blisters, mainly on my toes. I made the mistake of trying to make my old boots last for one additional trip. I should have invested in a new pair. The boots I wore had already done duty on half of the Appalachian Trail. The leather around the toes and lace eyelets was cracked, so even wet weeds soaked through the leather. Wet feet are a breeding ground for blisters. Plus my feet had grown from the pounding. Boots that felt fine when I first put them on, scrunched my toes as my feet swelled during the day. A good, well fitted pair of boots can make a world of difference in your comfort level while hiking.

Socks:

Two layers of socks help prevent blisters. The under layer should be a polypropylene liner sock designed to wick sweat away from your feet. The outer layer cushions your feet. Traditionally hikers have worn wool socks. They work well in cold hiking conditions. For summer hiking, they keep your feet too warm and increase sweating. We wear synthetic Trekking socks by Thorlo to give us padding without the added warmth. However, I recently read a sock test in *Backpacker Magazine* that recommended Expedition Trekking® socks by Smartwool. I plan to try them on my next hike.

Sleeping Pads:

To save weight (and money), we began the Appalachian Trail with three-quarter length, closed-cell foam pads by RidgeRest. In the cold weather of early spring, our feet froze at night, and we found the padding insufficient to give us a good night's sleep. So we switched to the full-length UltraLite® pads by Thermarest and now sleep warm and well. There are many Thermarest pads but be sure to get only the UltraLite® model or you'll lug unnecessary weight. The UltraLite® pad is a thin self-inflating air mattress, which is worth its weight in gold to a weary backpacker faced with a rocky tent site or a cold night.

Clothes:

We have one set of clothes that we hike in every day and another set of clothes that we sleep in and wear around town. We each hike in nylon shorts with built-in under pants, for all weather conditions except winter. If it's cold, we wear our gaiters for leg warmth. On top we wear polypropylene T-shirts. Polypropylene is far superior to cotton because it wicks moisture away from your body and dries quickly.   It comes in many brand names such as Duofold®, Capilene®, and MicroClimate®.   Polyester T-shirts would work well also.   In warm weather, I wear a synthetic jogbra rather than a T-shirt.

Our off-trail clothes are another set of shorts and polypropylene T-shirts.   For warmth we take nylon trail pants, turtleneck polypropylene shirts with long-sleeves and zipper fronts, and fleece jackets.   We also take along a second pair of socks so that we have dry socks for night.   If our hiking socks get wet, we continue to hike in wet socks until we can dry them in the sun.   If we swap wet socks for dry ones, we'll have two pairs of wet socks and cold feet at the end of the day.   For end-of-day walking and town days, we carry Teva®-like sandals.   They let your feet air out and promote foot health on the trail.   They're also useful if you have to ford any streams.

When hiking in colder weather, we also toss in a wool cap and fleece gloves for each of us.

Hiking Sticks:

We each use two sticks.   Rich has Leki hiking sticks, I use sawed-off ski poles.   Both suit the purposes of providing balance and taking pressure off of our knees.

Water:

Many hikers carry water filters, but they add weight, and

we've seen many of them break and clog in heavy trail use. We carry four Nalgene® bottles and iodine tablets. As long as you remember to rim each newly treated bottle of water, they're quite effective. Rimming is pouring some of the treated water around the threads and cap to rinse out untreated water. Some people find they dislike the iodine taste, but we don't even notice it.

However, along the Bruce Trail, a filter would probably be a good idea. Many of the water sources run through farmers' fields and pastures. A filter could eliminate pesticides and cryptosporidium as well as giardia. A good choice would be the PUR Hiker®. It's small and takes a beating with heavy trail use.

Bandannas:

These are a versatile hiking tool. We each carry two. Mostly we wear one as a headband and use the second to swab our sweaty faces. I've also used one to filter water, wear as a halter as I do the laundry, tie bread to the outside of my pack, serve as washcloth and towel, and wear as a sling if the need arises.

Cooking:

The predominate stove used by backpackers is the MSR Whisperlite®. It's a lightweight, reliable way to boil water. In case of trouble, however, we do carry a stove repair kit. We have two sizes of fuel bottles to use depending on the length of the trip and availability of fuel. Along the Bruce Trail, white gas fuel was available in small cans at most of the general stores. We carry a small butane lighter to light the stove. Attached to the draw string of our stove sack is a tiny military can opener.

We cook in a single stainless-steel cook pot with a cover that becomes a small pot when turned upside down. The pot is also our serving dish/plate. We each have one Lexan® spoon and a plastic cup.

Food:

Food is stored in a large draw-string stuff sack. To hang the food bag at night, we carry a thirty-foot length of parachute chord (available at sporting-goods stores) with an upside-down tunafish can placed six inches (15.2 cm) from one end. By hanging the food bag just below the tuna can, you prevent mice from traveling down the rope and helping themselves to your food.

Ditty Bags:

Each of us has a draw-string bag for miscellaneous stuff such as:

Mini Maglite® flashlights and headbands—Headbands that have Velcro® closures let you use the flashlight handsfree.

Toothbrushes and toothpaste—We use travel toothbrushes so that the bristles are covered in transit and the smallest tube of toothpaste that we can find.

Iodine tablets and white medical adhesive tape wound around the bottle

Multiple vitamins

Ibuprofen (painkiller that also reduces swelling)

Lip gloss with sunscreen (treatment for chapped lips)

Toilet paper rolled in small wads, minus the cardboard tube—The amount to take is a personal choice.

Q-Tips® cotton swabs

Maps and trail guides—We break them apart and put segments in each mail drop for only the area that we'll be hiking until the next mail drop.

A small paperback book—We tear the book apart and toss read sections in trash cans along the route, so that it becomes lighter as the trip goes on. Be sure to choose a small paperback book to begin with.

Moleskin® (felt pads with an adhesive backing which are available at any drugstore)—Use them to pad parts of the feet where friction causes soreness. A must for any hiker.

NewSkin® (a liquid, like clear nail polish, which you paint on blisters)—It dries to form a clear bandage which stays put on wet feet. Moleskin® and Band-Aid® adhesive strips slide off of wet feet and often cause additional blisters.

Dental floss and a needle—Use the floss for teeth and

also, with the needle, as a tough thread for repairing rips.

A few safety matches—(wooden matches with the heads dipped in wax) Use them for emergencies or if the small lighter runs out of fuel.

Two Band-Aid® adhesive strips for cuts—They're useless on sweaty feet. To bandage sweaty feet, I've had better luck making a square pad out of toilet paper and securing it with medical adhesive tape (that was rolled around the iodine tablet bottle).

A small pocket knife with built-in scissors and tweesers.

A small plastic comb

Tampons and panty liners

A tiny plastic bottle with an inch or two of Dr. Bronner's soap—This is a biodegradable soap, which we use mainly as shampoo at hostels. We do not use it in streams, lakes, or ponds. To wash our cook pot and cups, we use wet leaves, gravel, or sand and water, without any soap.

A small Walkman® radio with earphones

A small writing pad and lightweight pen

Nylon wallet carrying:

  Canadian traveler's checks—resupplied from each
    mail drop

  A few blank personal checks

  Some cash (Canadian)

Driver's licenses

Credit card

ATM card

Health insurance card

AAA card—Automobile Association of America card for possible motel discounts

A small list of addresses and emergency numbers of friends, family, and equipment vendors—You may need to write or call them.

Daily Routine

*J*ust as in civilized life, on the trail we evolved into patterns of behavior and responsibility. Rich and I never really discussed or planned who would be responsible for each task, but over time we fell into a daily routine to get the chores of hiking done efficiently. What it boiled down to was that I handled the inside tent chores and Rich handled the outside tent chores, with some exceptions. This division of labor may sound sexist, but we were doing the things that each of us enjoyed.

In the morning, Rich would be the first out of the tent (after all, he's the morning person). He'd retrieve the food bag and fix us Pop Tarts® toaster pastries and cups of cereal with rehydrated powdered milk. We'd eat breakfast, either inside the tent or out, depending on the weather. After breakfast, I'd stuff the sleeping bags into their sacks and deflate and roll the air mattresses. Meanwhile Rich would be working outside the tent, carrying our belongings from the tent and packing them into the appropriate backpack. I'd change into hiking clothes inside the tent, and Rich would change outside. Once I was done and emerged from the tent, we'd both collapse the tent and fold the tent poles. We'd then each finish packing our own backpacks and help each other hoist them into position on our backs.

We found it best to stop after one hour of hiking to consume a candy bar. This gave us a boost of energy to get through the morning. After that, we'd generally stop every two hours for another break. We carried munchies such as nuts, hard candy, red licorice, Tootsie Roll® pops, and granola bars in our belly pouches for these breaks.

When we found a campsite, we'd work together to erect the tent. Then I'd go inside to create a nest. Rich would stay outside, unpack the backpacks, and toss the in-tent stuff to me. I'd blow up the air mattresses, fluff the sleeping bags, zip them together, and arrange the rest of the stuff in an orderly fashion. Outside, Rich would prepare the cooking area and set up the stove. If we hadn't already done so on the way to the campsite, he'd go to retrieve water. Once done in the tent (and changed into campsite clothes), I'd exit the tent to sort food. Sorting food consisted of rounding up all the day's trash, pulling out the food for dinner, restocking our munchie bags, resupplying the lunch bag (which I carried), and segregating the breakfast food for easy access the next morning. While I did this, Rich would cook the various courses of our dinner.

After dinner, we'd hang the food bag, brush our teeth, make one last pit stop and head into the tent. Often this was before dark, so I'd read and Rich would listen to his radio. Sometimes we'd read aloud to each other. We always scanned the maps and trail guides, preparing for the next day's adventure.

No-trace Camping

Camping, or even hiking for that matter, along the Bruce Trail is a privilege granted by the generous people who own the land and those who manage the trail. As guests on private or public land, it's imperative that we follow a no-trace camping ethic. This means that after we have passed, there should be no evidence of our having been there. The components are simple:

•Stay on the established trails; do not cut switchbacks.

•Pick a campsite where you will not damage vegetation or disturb crops, young vegetation, and rare or sensitive vegetation.

•Camp in existing campsites whenever possible.

•Before you leave, scatter leaves, sticks, or whatever was natural on the site before you camped to make the site look unused.

•Use a backpacker's stove; do not build fires.

•Properly dispose of human waste away from water, trails, and campsites.

•Wash well away from campsites and water sources.

•Leave flowers, rocks, and other natural features undisturbed.

•Do not feed wildlife.

•Carry out everything you carry in (do not litter).

Meals

We are not gourmet chefs either on the trail or off. Particularly on the trail, we try to keep meals as simple as possible. The only meal we fire up the stove for is dinner. But, we do a fair amount of food preparation before a hike. First we remove excess packaging from each food item that we plan to take or ship in our mail drop. If necessary, we repackage food in Ziploc® bags. Whenever possible, we premix food items in ready-to-eat portions. For example, we add salt and powdered milk to a Ziploc® bag of instant potatoes. Here's a sampling of the foods we eat (not all in a single meal of course):

Breakfast:

Pop Tarts® toaster pastries

Dry cereal in rehydrated powdered milk (We tape a twist tie to the outside of the cereal bag so that we can close and reopen it.)

Trail Snacks:

Candy bars (especially Snickers®)

Granola bars

Red licorice sticks

Hard candies (in individual wrappers)

Tootsie Roll pops® (with the sticks cut short)

Beef jerky

Tang® instant orange drink

Peanut M&Ms®

Variety of nuts

Variety of seeds

Lunch:

>
> Bread (usually pita bread or bagels which we purchase along the way)
>
> Peanut butter
>
> Jelly (in a squeeze tube)
>
> Honey
>
> Dried black beans (We rehydrate them with hot water the night before in the empty peanut butter jar—excellent energy source.)
>
> Dried humus or garbanzo beans (Rehydrated with water at lunch time.)
>
> Dried fruits (apples, raisins, craisins, strawberries, blueberries, bananas)
>
> Pringles potato chips (in a can)
>
> Pretzels
>
> Cookies (especially ginger snaps)
>
> Variety of nuts

Dinner:

>
> Lipton noodle or rice dinners
>
> Macaroni and cheese
>
> Ramen noodles
>
> Dehydrated applesauce
>
> Spaghetti with dehydrated spaghetti sauce
>
> Dried vegetables (peas, carrots, corn, green beans, beets)
>
> Instant hot chocolate
>
> Jell-O® gelatin (drunk as a hot liquid)
>
> Instant cider
>
> Instant pudding (mix in water bottle)

Anytime Filler:

>
> Instant potatoes
>
> Instant oatmeal with raisins

Mail Drop Schedule

*H*ere is the list of our arrival at each mail drop. We mailed all of the boxes from Stoney Creek before starting the trip on August 13. Every box was at the post office waiting for our arrival.

Mail Drop	Arrival Date	Days to Next PO
Start at Queenston	August 13	5
Stoney Creek (L8G 2A1)	August 17	5
Kilbride (L0P 1G0)	August 22	3
Palgrave (L0N 1P0)	August 25	7
Ravenna (N0H 2E0)	September 2	4
Owen Sound (N4K 2K0)	September 6	3
Wiarton (N0H 2T0)	September 9	4
Lion's Head (N0H 1W0)	September 13	4
Tobermory	September 16	

Mail Drop Contents

Food is by far the largest component of the mail drops. In addition, we resupply things that we use up as we proceed, such as:

> Traveler's checks
> Writing notebooks for our journal
> Film
> Fresh socks once per month
> Pre-stamped postcards (to keep in touch back home)
> Toilet paper
> Maps and guide books for the next section
> Moleskin
> Bottles of iodine tablets with more white medical tape
> Liquid soap in small bottles
> Q-tips® cotton swabs
> Multiple vitamins
> Toothpaste
> Ibuprofen
> Tampons and panty liners
> DEET (added to the list after this hike)

In each mail drop box, we also include a large bubble envelope to mail home exposed film, written journals, maps, and any other items we decide we can live without.

Mail drop boxes are addressed to:
> General Delivery
> Your Name
> City, Province (State), Postal Code (Zip Code)
>
> Hold For Bruce Trail Thru-Hiker
> Expected Arrival Date: XXXXX XX

Definitions

B&B - abbreviation for bed and breakfast.

Blaze - a painted rectangular marking on a tree showing where the trail goes. Colors may be used to denote different trails. Blazes on the BruceTrail are white. Side trails are blue.

Brita® - the manufacturer of a popular home-water purifier.

Cairn - a pile of small rocks used to show the direction of the trail through terrain above tree level.

Cryptosporidium - a parasitic protozoa found in water which causes cryptosporidiosis, an intestinal disease.

Dolomite - a rock of calcium magnesium carbonate.

Dolostone - a carbonate sedimentary rock composed of fragmented or precipitated particles containing the material dolomite. Many dolostones have been altered from limestone.

Dump - a beach location where trees logged in the winter were taken and dumped into the water for transport by ship to mills.

Flowerpot - a towering rock formation with a limestone top and softer shale pedestal. They were formed by wave action eroding the escarpment.

Giardia - a parasitic protozoa (full name giardia lamblia) found in water that causes giardiasis, an intestinal disease.

Glacial pothole - formed during the Ice Age by water running over the edge of the glacier. The glacial melt water pushed hard granite rocks onto softer limestone acting as a type of grinding mill. The granite boulders still lie buried at the bottom of each cylindrical hole.

Gorp - any combination of trail munchies. A mixture of peanuts, raisins, and M&Ms® candy is a common gorp.

Karst - an area where water has dissolved the rock so that surface water can disappear underground.

Limestone - a rock of calcium carbonate.

NewSkin® - a clear liquid bandage manufactured by Medtech Labs, Inc., which is used to treat blisters.

Offset double blazes - two blazes where the top one is off center to show the direction of a turn along the trail.

PUD - a slang term of Appalachian Trail through-hikers meaning pointless ups and downs.

QEW - Queen Elizabeth Way, an expressway that runs from Buffalo, New York, to Toronto, Ontario.

R&R - a slang term for rest and relaxation.

Road allowance - a section of land reserved for future road development.

Sit-upon - a square of Tyvek® or oil cloth that you sit on, to keep clean and dry.

Stile - a wooden ladder or steps erected so hikers can climb over barbed-wire or electric fences.

Sundog - a light refraction (rainbow) at 22° on either side of the sun caused by light traveling through ice crystals in the upper atmosphere. Sundogs are quite rare.

Switchback - a trail section that loops back and forth across steep landscape to make the ascent/descent more gradual.

Talus - a collection of fallen, disintegrated, rocky material that has accumulated at the foot of a steep slope such as the face of the escarpment.

Trail magic - the name given to good deeds or special favors performed for long-distance hikers.

Tyvek® - a breathable moisture-barrier material used as a wrap in house construction. Hikers use Tyvek® as a ground cloth under tents and as sit-upons.

References

ALDHA (Appalachian Long Distance Hikers
Association)
10 Benning St., Box 224
West Lebanon, NH, USA 03784
email - aldha@connix.com

Bruce County Tourism
PO Box 180
33 Victoria Street North
Southampton, Ontario, Canada N0H 2L0
(800) 268-3838 from within Canada
email - brucetourism@sunsets.com

Bruce Peninsula National Park
PO Box 189
Tobermory, Ontario, Canada N0H 2R0
(519) 596-2233

The Bruce Trail Association (sells maps, trail guides,
and through-hiker's guide)
P.O. Box 857
Hamilton, Ontario, Canada L8N 3N9
(800) 665-HIKE from within Canada
(905) 529-6821

Grey Bruce Tourism
RR 5
Owen Sound, Ontario, Canada   N4K 5N7
(800) 265-3127 from within Canada
(519) 371-2071

Hike Ontario
Suite 411, 1185 Eglinton Avenue East
North York, Ontario, Canada M3C 3C6
(800) 422-0552 from within Canada

Niagara Escarpment Commission
232 Guelph Street
Georgetown, Ontario, Canada   L7G 4B1
(416) 877-5191

Index

Tuna Fish Can, 98, 196
Turbine, 31
Turtles, 85
Twelve Mile Creek, 35
Twin Flight Locks (see Locks)
Tyvek®, 188, 189-190, 208

𝒰

UltraLite Thermarest® Pads (see Sleeping
    Pads)
UNESCO, 15
Union Hill, 13
United Nations Educational, Scientific, and
    Cultural Organization (see UNESCO)
University of Guelph, 72
Upper Ordovician, 13
Urushiol, 75-76
USA Today, 64

𝒱

Vegetables, 57, 204
Velcro®, 191, 196
VIA, 55
Vibram (see Boots)
Village Restaurant, 170
Vineyards, 23
Virginia, 35, 89
Vitamins, 197, 206
Voles, 177

𝒲

Walkman® Radio (see Radio)
Wall-Rue Fern (see Ferns)
Wallet, 198
Water Bars, 42
Water Filter, 133, 194-195
Waterworks Road, 158
Waterdown, 62
    Waterdown Motel, 62
    Waterdown Taxi, 68
Waterwheel, 31
Webster Falls, 55, 56, 57
Wedding, 37
Welland, 25
Welland Canal, 10, 23, 24-25, 27, 28, 29, 42
Westhill Laundromat, 142
Wheat, 32, 104, 106
Whistle, 188
White Baneberry (see Flowers)
White Gas, 196
Wiarton, 155-156, 205
Wiggy's (see Sleeping Bag)
Wisconsin, 13, 14
Wizard Of Oz, 43
Wool Cap, 194
Wool Socks (see Socks)

Woolverton Mountain Road, 42
World Biosphere Reserve, 15, 16
Writing Notebook or Pad, 198, 206

𝒳, 𝒴

Yellow & Black Stripped Snake (see Snakes)
Yellow Clintonia (see Flowers)
Yews, 135
Yule, Don & Elizabeth, 141-142, 144, 146, 148-
    149

𝒵

Zip Lock® Bags, 203

We hope sharing our adventure inspires you to create
adventures of you own.

For more information explore our web site at:
www.footprintpress.com

Other Books Available from Footprint Press:

Take A Hike! Family Walks in the Rochester Area

by Rich and Sue Freeman

A practical guide to exploring Rochester, New York's 40+ trails and interesting places. Through maps and descriptions, this book shows where to take a stroll, walk the dog, or learn more about nature while having fun and learning local history.

ISBN # 0-9656974-6-0   US $16.95   Can $21.95

Take Your Bike! Family Rides in the Rochester Area

by Rich and Sue Freeman

Here are 29 possibilities for safe, mostly off-road, places to ride a bicycle around Rochester, New York. Enjoy the local history, pictures, and maps for each ride. Over 260 miles of fun and healthful adventures for all ages and abilities.

ISBN # 0-9656974-2-8   US $16.95   Can $21.95

Alter, A Simple Path to Emotional Wellness

by Judy Gurley

Alter is a manual which assists in recognizing and changing your emotional blocks and limiting belief systems. It uses easy-to-learn principles of biofeedback to retrieve subliminal information and achieve personal transformation.

ISBN # 0-9656974-8-7   US $16.95   Can $21.95

Order Form

Yes, I'd like to order Footprint Press books:

\#

___ **Take A Hike!** *Family Walks in the Rochester (NY) Area*

___ **Take Your Bike!** *Family Rides in the Rochester (NY) Area*

___ **Bruce Trail** - *An Adventure Along the Niagara Escarpment*

___ **Alter** - *A Simple Path to Emotional Wellness*

___ Total Books @ $16.95 US or $21.95 Can. each

For 1 or 2 books, add $3 per book for shipping and tax.
**Receive FREE shipping and tax when ordering
3 or more books.**

Total enclosed: $ _____

Your Name: _____

Address: _____

City: _____ State (Province): _____

Zip (Postal Code): _____ Country: _____

Make check payable and mail to:

Footprint Press
PO Box 645-R
Fishers, NY, USA   14453

Footprint Press Books are available at special discounts when
purchased in bulk for sales promotions, premiums, or fundraising.